"Change is inevitable. The question is, will you maximize the potential of change in your life? Rob's book will revolutionize your perspective toward change and its benefits. Start today, make a change, and dive into these practical, life-transforming truths."

—JOHN BEVERE
Author / Speaker
Messenger International, Colorado / Australia / United Kingdom

"*Change Before You Have To* is one of those books that you'll highlight, make notes in the margins, and refer back to time and again. The wisdom offered within its pages is timeless yet accessible to anyone. We have the power to do all things through Christ—including the act of making personal change. Rob offers the practical steps necessary to make such change a reality."

—DR. GEORGE O. WOOD
General Superintendent
The General Council of the Assemblies of God

"*Change Before You Have To* is a timely book that not only inspires us to make the changes necessary in order to run our race and finish our course, but also shows us how to do that. An invaluable addition to your bookshelf."

—CHRISTINE CAINE
Founder, A21 Campaign

"Having known Rob now for twenty-five years, I can say firsthand, he has lived out this book! Rob isn't just writing from a desk but from life experiences that he has captured for us in this incredible book that if applied will bring amazing changes to you as well. After reading this I'm changing now!"

—JOE CHAMPION
Lead Pastor, Celebration Church, TX

"The ability to change on purpose is a powerful gift from God. It's the number one thing that sets us apart, and it's the key to our success in every area of life. *Change Before You Have To* is one of those must-read books that will become a staple in your life, a resource you will use time and time again. For many years, I have personally known Rob, have seen his integrity and transparency in action both publicly and privately, and have been inspired by his tenacious will to embrace change. Do yourself a huge favor and get this book today!"

—LEE DOMINGUE
Founder of Kingdom Builders US & Trafficking Hope, Baton Rouge, LA

"In *Change Before You Have To*, Rob takes a 'slap you in the face with truth, then hand you a cup of hot cocoa' approach that is both refreshing and challenging like crazy! This book will cause readers to do what's right and best for their lives now instead of later. This book will change families, career paths, and destinies! Rob is a friend, a mentor, and most of all, Rob lives what he teaches."

—MATT KELLER
Lead Pastor, Next Level Church, Fort Myers, FL

"I learned long ago that change is here to stay! It is inevitable and necessary. So you better learn how to recognize and handle change. In this book, Rob clearly explains the 'what' and the 'how' involved in making personal change. It will help you handle the changes that you face."

—JOHN C. MAXWELL
Leadership Expert, Speaker, and *New York Times* Best-Selling Author

"This book will change your life. Rob makes his message of hope accessible to anyone—no matter where they are in life. This isn't a book full of Christian vocabulary and insider language. This is real talk about real change in a way that makes it relevant to your life right now."

—CHRIS HODGES
Pastor, Church of the Highlands
Author of *Fresh Air*

"Intrinsically built into the notion of change is the timing of change. On reflection of my over forty years of full-time Christian leadership, my greatest regrets are about not changing sooner rather than later. My change resistance, my change procrastination, my change rationalization slowed down my leadership journey. I know I would be further down the road had I read *Change Before You Have To* by Pastor Rob Ketterling. Forced change is simply a change of actions but change born out of understanding is transformational. To everyone desiring to lead transformational change, I recommend *Change Before You Have To*."

—DR. SAMUEL R. CHAND,
Author of *Cracking Your Church's Culture Code*
www.samchand.com

"Rob and his remarkable family blessed our family by staying with us for a few days while they were ministering to a local church. Our family was supernaturally touched, changed for the positive. We were privileged to see his family in real ministry action with the leadership of the local church in our living room. My companies have helped create ten thousand jobs in the past ten years by turning around difficult business situations. I wish I had Rob by our side in helping facilitate significant change because this is his gift from God."

—MICHAEL K. CLIFFORD
Educational Thought Leader
www.significantfederation.com
www.ministry.com

"It's so important to understand that we often need to make a change in our life now or pay the price later. Rob Ketterling has written a must-read book for anyone bold enough to make a change now. Read it, apply it, and your life will not be the same."

—STOVALL WEEMS
Lead Pastor, Celebration Church

"In this book Rob paints a picture that will help shift our thinking so we can approach change with a positive perspective. This book not only helps readers see the benefits of making proactive changes, but helps them know how to introduce healthy change into their lives. You're going to love it from cover to cover!"

—JOHN SIEBELING
Senior Pastor, The Life Church of Memphis

"Change is happening all the time, whether we like it or not. So why do so many of us try to avoid change? If you want to change but cannot, or even if you do not want to change (but need to!), Rob has written a book for everyone. Read this book and discover how you can embrace the changes you need to make."

—GREG SURRATT
Senior Pastor, Seacoast Church
Author of *Ir-Rev-Rend*

ROB KETTERLING

CHANGE

BEFORE
YOU HAVE TO

DISCOVER A NEW LIFE OF ABUNDANCE,
PASSION, & SATISFACTION

www.InfluencesResources.com

Published by Influence Resources
1445 N. Boonville Ave., Springfield, Missouri, 65802

Published in association with The Quadrivium Group—Orlando, FL
info@TheQuadriviumGroup.com
Developmental Editing—Ben Stroup, BenStroup.com—Greenbrier, TN
Copyediting, Proofreading, Interior Design—KLOPublishing.com
and Katherine@theDESKonline.com
Cover Design—Root Radius, LLC—Ackworth, GA

ISBN: 978-1-93783-052-6

Third printing 2013
Printed in United States of America

This book is dedicated to my wife, Becca,
who has loved me through all my changes.
Some bad, most good!
Thank you for helping me to change before I had to!
I love you!

CONTENTS

SECTION ONE—PREPARE TO CHANGE

The first step to making a change in our lives is to identify what needs to change. It's likely that we already know what those changes are yet we remain resistant for a variety of reasons. The power to change begins with the recognition that we can't stay the same.

SECTION TWO—FOLLOW THE PATH TO CHANGE

Change is hard because it asks us to alter our habits. We must leave behind what is comfortable today before we can establish a new normal in our lives. When we gain clarity around what we value, the path to change becomes clear.

SECTION THREE—OVERCOME THE OBSTACLES TO CHANGE

Change does not come without challenges, which is why some people never change. We should expect to experience resistance. Our resolve to continue moving toward change is equal to our clarity about the need to change.

SECTION FOUR—PUT ON THE MIND OF CHANGE

God gives us the strength to change. When we renew our thinking and refocus our attention on eternal things, it influences every other area of our lives. The change we strive to make becomes possible as we bring our lives into harmony with what matters to God.

ACKNOWLEDGMENTS

To my wife Becca—you are the love of my life, I would change over and over for you!

To my boys, Connor and Logan—I love you and love being your dad. I hope these changes let me spend many more years with you!

To my parents—Mom, you're still here to read this and you need to know, you and Dad taught me so much. You two have been amazing. I love you!

To everyone at River Valley Church—I love our church, the staff, the Elders, the Deacons. It's a privilege to do life together and lead people to an authentic relationship with Jesus Christ! I'm grateful for your over-and-above work on this book!

To the team at Influence—thanks for believing in me! Steve and Susan Blount, Eliza, Trevor, (others on team)—we did it! You guys were so easy to work with.

To my writer Ben Stroup—you made this book better than I could have on my own. Thank you for helping me learn the ropes! You got my heart on the page!

To my trainer Steve Toms—thank you for motivating me to change and keep the change! See you at 7:00 a.m.!

To Justin Lathrop—your networking got me to the right people at Influence. Who do I need to meet next? Thank you!

FOREWORD

The single most important characteristic about human life is having the capacity to change. When we stop changing, we die. It's that simple. Unfortunately, many people—even those who believe in Jesus—don't believe they have the capacity for change. They know they need to, but they often feel powerless to change.

I've seen this attitude time and again throughout my ministry. People who find a life full of abundance, passion, and satisfaction are people who believe in the power of change. They improve their minds, change their habits and decisions, and put into action what they believe to be true.

Rob is the real deal. He has lived what he talks about in this book. I've seen him make tough decisions throughout our friendship that have inspired some changes in my own life. What I love most about Rob is that he believes what he writes about.

Like Rob, I believe change is possible for you too. It starts with recognizing the change you need to make, choosing to take the steps necessary for the change to take place, and then keeping the change and choosing not to slip back into your old habits and hang-ups. When we believe that real change is possible, we experience a power and confidence that will carry us through the changes we need to make today.

This book will be one that you keep close by and refer to when you doubt change is possible. Go through it with a few close friends who share your same desire to reach for more than just an ordinary life, too.

Read this book. It will give you the tools to make the changes you know you need to make. Stop waiting for the right time, circumstances, or opportunity. The window of opportunity is now.

—MARK BATTERSON
Lead Pastor, National Community Church, Washington, D.C.,
and author of *The Circle Maker*

"People who live in a state of *vulnerability*
need to change to *stability*
so they can really live when they change
to a state of *vitality*!"
—STEVE TOMS (My Trainer)

INTRODUCTION

Change before you have to. Think about it. Do people really do that? You probably have a sense of something in your life you'd like to change. The mere fact that you picked up this book and turned a few pages in tells me that you're curious, which means you're wondering if the things you've been wanting to change about yourself, your family, your job, etc., are possible. Let me cut to the chase: Whatever it is you want to change is possible, and the life you've always wanted is within your reach. It really is.

Change is so worth it, but it's scary. Most people approach the idea of change with anxiety, frustration, and resistance. Change means we must admit that something in our life hasn't measured up to what we think it could or should be.

For some people, the decision not to change could result in significant, even life or death, circumstances. But for most people, the changes we want to make are subtle and somewhat under the radar. In fact, most people who don't know us very well may not even recognize some of the things we want to change about ourselves or our circumstances. Without making the change, however, we must settle for a life that falls short of our expectations. That's not my hope for you. That's not God's hope for you either.

God did not promise to give us only life. He promised life with all the abundance and fullness He intended from the very beginning of creation. That promise is available to you today, if you choose to change.

I remember a recent conversation that led to significant change in my life. It is so clear in my mind, as if it happened yesterday. My wife and I were on a double date with some really close friends. It was a normal dinner as we talked about all sorts of things. Mostly, we were catching up on children, family, ministry, and life in general. Then the topic shifted. What happened next, no one could have predicted.

I was commenting on how lost my friend would be if he lost his wife and began ribbing him about being high maintenance when he turned the attention to me. My friend commented that I'd be no different and would be completely lost if Becca, my wife, suddenly wasn't in my life. I completely agreed.

But I didn't leave it there. (Man, I wish I would have!) Next, I said, "If I lost Becca, I'd have to lose some weight."

Of course, Becca happened to hear that last line loud and clear. She responded curiously, "What's that?" In that moment I was looking for an escape hatch but my friend wasn't about to let me find it.

He blurted out, "What he means is that if something happened to you and he had to go back on the market, he couldn't attract a woman like you looking like he does." With friends like that, who needs enemies?

Let me first say, I'm so grateful for all the change that statement has brought into my life, but in that moment I wanted to die.

Have you ever had one of those experiences where you said something and then realized the full weight of what you just said? That's what happened to me. Before I realized what came out of my mouth, I started recounting the different changes I'd have to make in my life if I had to start dating again.

This stunning revelation bubbled up in the midst of my rambling. To, be honest, I couldn't believe how casual I was about it. I admitted that I'd have to lose some weight, get back in shape, and start taking better care of myself all the way around.

There is nothing that unusual about change like that. We've all seen others change because of a wakeup call. Honestly, it's a goal many people share. This statement was particularly controversial because I said this as I was imagining life after the unfortunate death of the love of my life. Yes, even pastors say things they wish they could take back. Honestly, I still can't believe I said it.

What had been a light-hearted topic of discussion between two guys now became a serious topic of conversation among the four of us. (You know where this is going, don't you?)

Without missing a beat, Becca interrupted and asked one of those questions that only a wife could ask: Why would you choose to make those changes for a woman you have yet to meet—and may never meet—when you could make those changes for the love of your life today?

It was a question that sliced through the joking and the laughs and actually struck a chord within my soul. There was no way out of this one. I had dug my hole, and I needed to get comfortable. I'm a professional communicator, but nothing in my ministry or preaching prepared me for what to say in this moment. I was going to have to answer her question because all eyes were on me.

Becca was right to wonder why I was willing to make those changes in order to meet a fictitious woman following a terrible tragedy when my wife—the love of my life and a woman way out of my league—was right in front of me today. It was one of those guy moments when you realize that what you just said cost you something, and it might be at a jewelry store or even worse. There was no going back.

So what was my friend doing while Becca was pressing in for the kill? Of course, what any good friend would do. He was cheering her on. I gave him this look to encourage him to let it go, but it was clear that I had found myself in the midst of an opportunity to either redeem myself or forever be haunted by my big mouth. There had to be a guy code or something he was violating.

You've all had a similar experience. Somebody casually said something. You read a billboard. A song caught your attention. Whatever it was, it came upon you in a flash and left just as quickly as it came. You wondered what it might be like to make a few changes. Even more important, you wondered if your life today is as good as it gets. If you're honest with yourself, life hasn't exactly lived up to your expectations.

But then you talk yourself out of the change you know you need to make. You convince yourself that change is possible for other people but not for you. Not true!

I am convinced that the reason you picked up this book is that you're not presently experiencing the life of abundance, passion, and satisfaction that you had hoped for. Something isn't right. You know it, but you're not sure what to do next. Your friends and family have offered their advice, but you've haven't acted on their suggestions.

You just keep pressing on hoping that it will get better. Or worse, you decide that you need to change but you choose to wait for a future event that will somehow make the necessary change much easier to process, digest, and implement. The perfect time to make a change is not sometime in the future but now. Today is all we're guaranteed. Tomorrow may not come.

Maybe you scan the TV channels, listen to a motivational speaker, attend an inspirational event, or go to church every now and then with hopes of hearing someone on a platform talk about the abundant life, a better life. You wonder whether your life really can be better than it is today or if change is only possible for other people—pretty people, rich people, or powerful people. What about ordinary people? Is there hope for the rest of us, too?

Knowing you need to change but not knowing the next step can be an overwhelming place to be. When you know you can't stay the same, you are left with only one decision: adjust to a more sustainable, healthy lifestyle or expect more of the same. The reason I believe you don't attempt change is because you don't feel strong enough or confident enough in your ability to get to the other side of change successfully.

The good news is that there is a way to make the changes you want in your life and begin living a life of abundance, passion, and satisfaction. It's possible. I believe God wants you to experience life in all its fullness. Now let me explain that last sentence. Even if you are not a Christian, I make no apologies for this statement. For change to be possible in your life, you must have faith. That's what makes change possible. Without faith, you won't have the power to create any type of lasting change, and that necessary faith is only available through God's grace.

Authentic change isn't something that happens for a season; it's a commitment to undoing a habit or hang-up that has subtly crept in and become part of how you do life. The problem is rarely big enough in the beginning to be a concern. It isn't until you realize your pants don't fit, your marriage is almost over, or your mind isn't clear until you down your first drink of alcohol that you are forced to deal with change.

> Change occurs at the intersection of hope and opportunity.

What if you took a completely different posture to the change you know you need to make in your life? What if you decided to change *before* you had to instead of *because* you had to? What if you would embrace the opportunity today to begin living a life full of abundance, passion, and satisfaction? You can!

The challenge for you is this: do you really want a better life, or are you satisfied with what you have today? If you are satisfied with living a life that is less than what God wants for you, then put this book down, use it as a doorstop, and stop wasting your time. What I'm about to reveal to you is a process that will empower you to identify the change you need to make, provide a path to change, and help you keep the change process in your life moving forward.

This is a book about action. Change occurs at the intersection of hope and opportunity. If you're not willing to take action, then this book isn't for you. You'll be sorely disappointed.

If however, you are ready to take the next step, then keep reading. What is about to be revealed to you will unlock the path you've been searching for. It leads to the life you've always wanted but thought was out of your reach. This is not an empty promise, but it is only available to those who are willing to bring their thinking, believing, and actions in harmony with the eternal truth revealed in God's Word and change before they have to.

Change won't be easy, but it will be worth it once you get to the other side. Nothing will be the same from this day forward. Today is the first day of the rest of your life and the day to make the change you want to see take place in your life.

SECTION ONE

PREPARE TO CHANGE

Chapter 1

ADMIT YOU NEED
TO CHANGE

I've always been a thin person. Eating whatever I wanted was part of my life. I really never had to think about it. If I wanted it, I ate it. Being hungry wasn't even a requirement. Living (and eating) that way worked for me for most of my life. That is, it worked until it didn't.

Along the way, I didn't think much about my weight gain. I mean, that's a normal part of life, right? Who doesn't add on a few pounds over time?

Then one conversation changed everything. Following that dinner conversation, I decided to make a change. In my mind, there was no going back. It was a turning point where I had to face the reality that my eating habits, physical fitness, and weight gain needed to be dramatically adjusted.

When I finally faced the music and realized I needed to change, I had to come to grips with how out of control my life had become in the area of food. Let me be clear: I'm a very disciplined person. I'm faithful in so many areas. I think this is one way that I let myself get by with an undisciplined approach to food. We all are allowed our indulgences, right? No one wants to go through life looking like they are sucking on a lemon. Of course not!

I was tired of my jeans feeling snug, having to wear my XL shirts untucked (and not just because it's cool and casual), and getting out of breath going up a short flight of stairs. My decision to let food rule me certainly came with some instant satisfaction. Ultimately, it was limiting me in so many other ways.

The question I want you to chew on is this: What is limiting your life today? Until you come to grips with the things in your life that are controlling you, you won't be able to change. It may have been a dinner conversation that became the catalyst for the change in my life, but the truth is, I had been unwilling to admit I needed to change for some time.

Life was moving along. Everything else seemed to be going so well that it was easy for me—and others around me—to give me a "get out of jail free" card. But I knew deep down inside that I had to take control, recognize what was limiting me, and admit I needed to make a change.

I'm so thankful I was able to get to this point of decision without a tragic event like a heart attack, stroke, or other major medical complication. I could have easily been writing this from a wheelchair or hospital bed. But I chose to admit that I needed to change before I had to instead of waiting until I had no other option.

> Until you come to grips with the things in your life that are controlling you, you won't be able to change.

The date was November 14. I decided to start my journey by getting a reality check of just how bad my health was. I knew I wouldn't be able to track my progress without a baseline, so I met with my doctor to check my cholesterol, weight, and to discuss next steps. His assessment revealed that my cholesterol was 250 (not a misprint), and I was almost forty pounds overweight. Wow! I must have missed high cholesterol and weight gain warning labels on those Little Debbie snack cakes.

I told my doctor I wanted to be treated like a heart attack patient. I wanted to be proactive and aggressive. He gave me the green light to start exercising, so my next step was to actually go to the health club where I was a member and talk to a nutritionist, develop a plan with a trainer, and start making change a reality.

To be honest, I live a public life. No, I'm not a celebrity. I'm not famous. But I'm a pastor of a church of approximately five thousand people. That means I regularly speak to large groups. It's a lot of fun until you realize your personal life—to a certain degree—is on stage, too. That means your successes are shared along with your failures. It also means I have the opportunity to share my experience with others in a way that might encourage them to make a change.

Publicly admitting my need to change cost me. It cost me my pride. I wanted to believe I had it all together. This is tough, especially for guys. We feel like if we just keep moving forward life will work out the details in our wake. Only, it rarely happens that way. Most of the time it's what we choose to ignore that ends up unraveling all that we've been striving for and working to achieve.

Dealing with my pride was just the beginning. It turned out that overcoming pride was easy in comparison to the reality that admitting my change also meant I would have to stick with it, until I—and everyone else paying attention—started to see some measurable change. Honestly, that whole experience was embarrassing. I wanted to tell others about it, but I also wanted to avoid the disappointment some might have in me for getting to the point where I had to make such a dramatic change.

I remember the feedback I received after I publicly admitted I needed to make a change. Someone told me, "Really? Pastor Rob, you're so disciplined in every area of your life. You have a great marriage, great kids, and you've got your spiritual life going on. Yet you missed it big time in the area of being physically fit." What they really thought was that because I was a pastor, I was above being addicted to anything. Not true. Addiction is addiction. And I was addicted to having second and third helpings, lying around, and munching on Little Debbie snack cakes.

Others said things like, "Wow, I'm fatter than you, and my cholesterol is lower than yours. You must really be in bad shape." I couldn't quite figure out whether or not this person was trying to encourage me or was proving to me he had figured out a way for me to be healthy and not make the change I had just announced on the platform. I just smiled and agreed.

I'm telling you this because I want to be transparent with you. I want to be honest. Very few people in my life are completely honest with me. Telling others about my decision reinforced my own commitment to change, and it created a level of accountability through expectation that wouldn't let me quit.

I was going to need all the strength and encouragement I could get to make it to the other side of change. Having that was the only assurance I had that I would stick with my decision long enough to create the change I needed in my life. It's likely the same for you, too.

Maybe you can wear a short sleeve shirt, your biceps are just bulging, your body fat is 8 percent, and your cholesterol is 160. Maybe you can eat food all day long, and it doesn't affect you. Maybe you're great. But you know what? Maybe your marriage is a wreck. And *that's* the area you're hoping nobody notices.

Again, you may act like you have it all going on but right now your life is falling apart in one or more areas. Maybe I covered up my fat by untucking my shirt, but you're likely covering up some areas of your life, too. The book of Proverbs says, "Even a fool is thought wise if he keeps silent" (17:28). So you just kind of nod your head, go on about your life, and hope no one notices the changes you need to make in your life.

> You can either change *because* you have to or you can change *before* you have to.

And I think it's time for you to get honest with yourself and those you love. I think it's time for you to admit there are areas of your life you have not changed that you need to change. And you can either change *because* you have to or you can change *before* you have to.

It's your call. I just know that changing before I had to was way easier than dealing with the change because I had to. Don't let fear, pride, embarrassment, or someone else's expectations keep you from admitting to yourself and others the things in your life that are limiting you and holding you back from the life you've always wanted.

CHAPTER 1 IN REVIEW

Key Ideas

- Change is a personal decision.

- Admitting the need to change is the first step to creating change.

- You can change before you have to or because you have to.

- Pride can keep you from changing because you want to protect the impression of a perfect life.

- Everyone has something in their life that is limiting them from something better.

Discussion Questions

1. List three things in your life that are holding you back. These can be about your career, family, or personal habits.

2. Why is it hard to admit the need to change?

3. Describe a time when you talked yourself out of changing something about yourself because you compared yourself to someone else.

4. When was the last time you had a checkup with your doctor? Is there a change an expert has advised you to make that you're ignoring?

5. Who do you need to tell about your need to change to hold yourself accountable to actually make the change?

Chapter 2

STOP PLAYING
THE CHANGE GAME

No one gets excited about change. Don't believe me? Just try to change something—even if it's minor—and watch how people react.

Put the kid's toys in a different room, change the paint color on your walls (without telling your spouse first), or start buying a diet version of your favorite soda from the grocery store and watch the faces of your family turn as the level of groaning rises. We might be convinced that if we made little changes they wouldn't matter much to us, but we are kidding ourselves. We like what we like, and we like what we like in the way we like it.

In the same way, life is a series of systems and processes. As long as those systems and processes play out in the way we anticipated, we're good. Everyone has preferences and prescriptions for how we like things to be and to be done. When we are confronted with the possibility of the need to change those systems and processes, we have a tendency to react swiftly and defensively.

Churches are usually not excited about change. You change the worship style or order of the service and everyone notices. Some say, "Whoa! Whoa!

Whoa! What was that? Why did we do that? I didn't like that song. It's a new song. Whoa! What happened to my favorite song?" Ever been in the middle of one of those conversations? I have. It's not pretty, and it often becomes personal.

One time I remember we changed how we set up the chairs. We did "church in the round," which means we moved the platform to the middle of the room and placed the chairs around it. It was an experiment, but it threw everybody off. Many responded, "Oh no! I don't like that. We can't do that, can we?"

People don't like change at their place of business either. Management says, "Oh, the Union will never go for the change!" The Union says, "Management will never go for that kind of change!" And most people walk around at work saying, "It's not my job! I'm not changing. It's not my job. What's my job? I'm doing my job."

We don't like change. And it's time for us to realize that change is inevitable. Every one of us has to change. We're not to stay put. We're to be moving forward and changing—always. Change is inherent to life, but we often work very hard to avoid change at all costs. This is what I like to call: Playing the Change Game.

One of the things I remember the doctor telling me was how difficult it is for people to change even when they are suffering from the effects of what they need to change. For example, my doctor told me that he would take smokers around the hospital and show them the horrible things that might happen to them if they continued to smoke. The experience would be an eye opening one, for sure. But the doctor admitted that it rarely created true, lasting change.

I was curious as to why not. It would seem to me that people would see the effects smoking can have on their lives and stop. Watching someone breathe through a tube, talk through an electronic voice box, or lose a lung would certainly motivate me to make a change if I were a smoker. Nevertheless, many continue to choose to smoke. The potential cost for not changing this habit is high, and that's not accounting for death.

The doctor admitted that the experience usually garnered a tear or two and a verbal acknowledgement that the person would start to make changes to avoid the painful effects. The doctor admitted he had little hope for most patients. Now I would think that a doctor would be the most optimistic person in the room. It finally hit me. He's had the same conversations with the same people over and over again. Some who took the tour with him are now exhibits for new "tourists." The doctor knew that the change would never be lasting until the patient stopped playing the change game and decided to make adjustments.

I want to look at someone in the Bible who refused to change. His name was Pharaoh. You can read the actual account in Exodus 7–14. I'm just going to summarize the story here.

The Israelites became God's chosen people, and while they were captive in Egypt, they were slaves to Pharaoh, the ruler of Egypt. Pharaoh took advantage of them and made them do hard labor.

> Change is inherent to life, but we often work very hard to avoid change at all costs.

As they were working, God sent a deliverer named Moses. God said to Moses, "You are going to go to Pharaoh, and you are going to tell him that I want him to set my people free. I want them to be able to leave and go to the land that I have promised to them. And they're going to leave and go to that land; Pharaoh has to let them go. He can change before he has to."

And so Moses went to Egypt to talk to Pharaoh. He said, "God wants you to let His people go. It's time. He sent me to tell you. He wants them to go."

And Pharaoh predictably said, "No, I'm not going to let them go."

Pharaoh's decision not to listen to Moses came with consequences. His decision resulted in a succession of ten plagues. First, all the water in Egypt turned to blood. Pharaoh responded, "I don't care. It doesn't matter. I'm still not letting God's people go."

So God said, "Alright. Here's another plague that's going to come along." And He filled the land full of frogs. Frogs were everywhere.

And Pharaoh said, "I'm not letting them go."

And then God sent another plague. Gnats and flies, and on and on. All these plagues kept coming. And in the process, Pharaoh refused to change his mind. God wanted Pharaoh to change. He tried to get his attention, but Pharaoh never responded.

By the way, God has a way of getting you to change. He just does. It may be through a conversation like mine, a particular experience or circumstance, or even a book like this one. When you do recognize the need to change, you have to decide to pay attention or ignore the warning signs. One response leads to abundance, passion, and satisfaction, and the other leads to more of the same.

In the midst of all this back and forth, Pharaoh played the change game. And we play the change game all the time too. We tell ourselves, "I'm going to change. I'm going to do this. I'm going to do it differently. Today will be different!" And by lunch that day, it's no different. Ever been there? Me too! This really is pride keeping us from change.

Pharaoh started to wear down. He said to Moses, "Okay, Moses. I need these things that are happening to stop. How about this? You know, you really just want to go to your land to worship God. How about if you just worship God here? How about if you just worship God here, and you don't go there? I'm feeling bad about this, so I'm changing my mind. I'm going to let you worship here."

Moses said, "No, nada, not gonna happen. We are not worshipping here. We're worshipping there on our Promised Land, and we're leaving."

Pharaoh's decision not to go along with God's plan resulted in a couple more plagues. Pharaoh continued playing the change game. He wanted to change, but only on his terms.

Pharaoh said, "Okay. How about if I just let the men go? You leave the women and the children here, and just the men go and worship. I think I can just let the men go."

And Moses shook his head and said, "No, we're not doing that."

So Pharaoh said, "Okay, I'm not doing that. Keep on being slaves."

As a result of Pharaoh's continued resistance, God sent more plagues. Pharaoh finally said, "Okay, okay. This time I realized I've sinned." He even said the right words. "This time I know that I've sinned, and I've done wrong. Here's what I'll do for you Moses: Go ahead and take the men, the women, and the children, but leave all your livestock here."

Then comes the famous line from Moses: "No! We are not leaving one hoof left behind. We're taking it all!"

How many of you would like Moses to negotiate for you? I would! Most of us would take Pharaoh's offer and run. Moses said, "We're not leaving one hoof behind; we are going for it!"

Pharaoh responded, "No, no, no. I'm not going to change my mind."

Finally, God sent the angel of death one night and struck the firstborn male of every Egyptian household.

That event broke Pharaoh. He finally said, "Okay, go! Go! Go! Your men, your women, your children, all your livestock. Take it! Go! Here's some other stuff. Go! Get out of here!"

And so the children of Israel left Egypt after almost four hundred years of slavery. As they left, they got to the Red Sea. There was no way around, so God parted the Red Sea, and they walked across on dry land.

Pharaoh was so upset and so angered about this, he pursued the Israelites. He led his army into the water. Only, Pharaoh hadn't changed but was just playing the change game. He was obsessed with what had happened to him, and he didn't like the change.

Pharaoh and his army pursued the Israelites without giving much thought to their own safety. He was so mad he couldn't see straight. The Bible says that God—in that moment—caused the water to cover him. Pharaoh and his army drowned.

Here was a guy playing the change game. "Oh, I changed! I changed!" Pharaoh compromised a little but never really changed completely. Even to the point of his own death, he resisted change.

When I think about Pharaoh's actions, I just want to look at him and say, "Crazy Pharaoh! Why couldn't you get it? You were messing with God. God wanted you to change and you wouldn't do it. Crazy Pharaoh! Why wouldn't you change?"

And then I look at us and say, "Crazy us." We don't change. We won't change. We avoid change. We get to a certain point, and we don't change anymore. We avoid it. I keep thinking, why don't we change? We know that we're supposed to change. We know we have bad habits. We know we're supposed to get rid of these things. On an even deeper level, we know we have sin and things that hinder us in our walk with God, yet we don't change! Why is that?

It's easier to play the change game. It's like getting close enough to the edge of a cliff to look down and see the water below but never actually jumping off. We experience part of the adrenaline rush, but we never really get to experience the rush that comes from jumping off the edge and splashing into the water. When you only see the impact the change could make in your life but never make the change, you cheat yourself out of a life that is much more than you ever thought it could be.

If you've admitted the need to change, you've likely thought about the steps needed to actually make the change. You psych yourself up through conversations and self-talk. You might have even prayed about it. You honestly believe that you can change and want to change. But when it comes down to making a different decision in that moment, you slip back into your old habits and hang-ups yet again.

> The only path to something different includes change. Don't be a casualty of the change you refuse to make.

True change is never accomplished by playing the change game. Sooner or later our never-ending efforts to avoid change will catch up to us through the effects of the change we refuse to make. Just like the doctor noted, sometimes the patients he takes as tourists through the hospital in hopes to create change in their lives, end up being the people in the tour itself.

Stop fooling yourself because you're not fooling anybody else. You were made for a life of abundance, passion, and satisfaction. You will only experience more in this life when you choose to remove the limits you have placed upon yourself. The only path to something different includes change. Don't be a casualty of the change you refuse to make.

CHAPTER 2 IN REVIEW

Key Ideas

- Everyone has preferences and prescriptions for how we like things to be and to be done.

- Change is inherent to life, but we often work very hard to avoid change at all costs.

- God has a way of getting us to change.

- It's easier to play the change game than to actually make a change.

- When you do recognize the need to change, you have to decide to pay attention or ignore the warning signs. One response leads to abundance, passion, and satisfaction, and the other leads to more of the same.

Discussion Questions

1. In thirty words or less, how would you define what it means to play the change game?

2. What are the telling signs someone is playing the change game? Give real-life examples.

3. Why do you think we work so hard to avoid change rather than make the change?

4. How do our preferences play into our resistance to change?

5. Is there something in your life today that is causing you to play the change game? If so, what? How will you respond differently?

Chapter 3

UNDERSTAND WHY YOU AVOID CHANGE

People avoid change. We don't see what we don't want to see. We don't hear what we don't want to hear. We don't speak what we don't want to speak. It's our way of resisting the change in our lives we so desperately need to make.

I'm not suggesting your life is miserable, falling apart, or that you are in the middle of some type of crisis. You may or may not be. That's not the point. What I think you should be aware of is that every person is resistant to change—even the change they know they need to make.

It's easier to identify and make changes when you have to. What I want to highlight is that more often than not, the changes we need to make are below the surface of our lives. These, by the way, can also be the most deadly. There are no perfect people. People who act or appear perfect scare me because I wonder what is brooding below the surface.

No lightning bolt is going to strike you down if you don't change. If you stop reading this book now, no harm will come to you as a result of it. Nevertheless, whatever you are refusing to change is limiting you in a very specific way. That won't change—even if you stop reading this book. Avoiding change will certainly keep you from living a life of abundance, passion, and satisfaction.

It's rare that we don't see or sense the need to change within us; it's more likely that we refuse to admit what we know to be true. We convince ourselves that what we need to change really isn't that bad anyway. We rationalize away any ideas we might have about personal change. I think we do this for a variety of reasons.

> Every person is resistant to change—even the change they know they need to make.

Some of us avoid change because of fear. We'd rather deal with what we know and what is familiar to us than struggle through and endure change. Change is a lot of work. Period. There is no way around it. But I can assure you that the energy we use to avoid change is as much if not more than the energy needed to change.

Fear is an interesting emotion. There is good fear. This is what psychologists call the "fight or flight" mechanism. It is a part of the human psyche that defends us from danger and provides an instant response to protect ourselves when danger arises. There is another dimension of fear that holds us back because we fear the price of change is greater than the cost of staying the same—even if staying the same is less than what we had first hoped for.

That second dimension of fear is the very reason so many people I meet with don't want to work on their marriage, learn a new skill, change careers, grow spiritually, or begin exercising. When we start to think in terms of change, there is a part of our minds that we go to battle with. We have to fight the ideas that combat the change we want to make. Fear is the source of this resistance.

Another reason so many people avoid change is discouragement. Some of us are discouraged about change because it doesn't happen fast enough. Do you know how many one-day diets I did? Too many to count!

I told myself regularly, "Today I'm changing! I'm going to lose weight!" And at the end of the day I'd look at the same face in the mirror and think to myself, "I didn't lose any weight!" What's worse, sometimes I'd gain weight! So it was easy to say, "That's over! Done with that!" Each time that happened, it was easier for me to avoid the change than deal with my avoidance of it.

When I seriously decided to make a change, I changed. As a result of my personal resolve, I've stayed with it. I was able to lose weight, gain muscle, wear a medium-sized shirt, and lower my body fat. That kind of change is possible for you too. Just because I'm a pastor doesn't mean I'm superhuman. I promise you that's not the case. I'm really no different from you.

But we become discouraged when the change doesn't happen fast enough in our lives. Guys are really prone to this. We pump ourselves up by saying, "Let's change! Right now!" Then our wives say, "Well, it's going to take months." We say, "Months? It's been three minutes! We just decided to change, right? So that means we've changed, right?" And she rolls her eyes and says, "Not exactly."

A third reason people avoid change is rebellion. I'm not talking about what your teenagers do when they don't pay attention to you. Rebellion is simply refusing to do what we know we should do because of pride or selfishness.

Refusing to change allows the opportunity for pride to get in the way. (Remember Pharaoh?) We tell ourselves and others that this is just the way it is. We say things like, "My whole family is like that. It's in my blood." Or we excuse our behavior by saying, "I'm *this* or *that*. And that's the way it's gonna be."

Another common form of rebellion is refusing to forgive someone when we know we should. I'll never forget the lady who sat next to me on the plane on the way to San Diego. She said, "I'm from Canada, but I am flying to San Diego. I'm going to Mexico for treatment because I have these growths and ulcers in me, and the doctors are confounded by it. They don't know what it is."

As she talked, the direction of the conversation changed dramatically. Her story flowed. She said, "You know what? I hate my ex-husband. He did me so wrong. I hate him. I'll never forgive him. And I also hate my parents.

I can't stand what they did to me. My dad abused me. I hate him, and I hate my neighbor."

No matter how I tried to comfort her, she had an angry response. You can guess how excited I was to get off that plane. How sad for her, and how sad for you if that is your life and perspective. It doesn't have to be like that.

As she laid out all the junk in her life, I kept thinking that perhaps her attitude and outlook on life should be part of her treatment plan. I told her, "Choosing not to forgive someone can kill you. If you want freedom, you need to forgive those people."

And she said, "I can't forgive them." The reality was she preferred to carry hate around in her mind and heart than to let it go. She knew it was the only path to true health but she refused to take that step. She was rebellious. Even when confronted with the truth, she would not change.

A fourth reason some of us don't change is we are just flat-out lazy. The thought of reading the Bible, working out, planning a date night, or committing to doing anything consistently is too overwhelming to even consider. You might be saying to yourself, "Come on, Pastor Rob. Every day? Every single day? Doesn't that sound a little ambitious?"

Yes. Change is ambitious. Change is constant. And change only happens for those who are ready to go "all in" for something greater than what they have today.

A fifth reason some avoid change is we are procrastinators. Tomorrow is always the day everything starts. How many diets start on Monday or in January? We decide that we'll focus on our marriage after we get our promotion. We put off what we know we need to do for a variety of reasons. We spend more time creatively coming up with reasons to avoid changing rather than just doing it.

Nothing will change until we decide to change. And deciding to decide tomorrow is not a valid decision. When people say they'll change tomorrow, they never change. Be honest. You know exactly what I'm talking about. When we use words and phrases like "tomorrow," "the next day," or even "someday soon," those days and moments never seem to come around. The time to change is *now*.

People who avoid change do so because they refuse to face the truth of their situation. I'm not going to help you uncover any new excuses in this book. You already know what they are, and you already know what excuses you've been using to avoid change in your life.

> People who avoid change do so because they refuse to face the truth of their situation.

Admitting to your avoidance strategy is the first step to ushering in change into your life, your marriage, your job, and your family. You're going to hear the truth in this book. You're going to learn how to change. The question is what will be your decision: will you choose to change, or will you continue to avoid change?

CHAPTER 3 IN REVIEW

Key Ideas

- People are skilled at avoiding change.

- It's rare that we don't know at least one thing we need to change about our lives; it's more likely that we refuse to admit what we know to be true.

- Often the changes we avoid are the ones that lie just below the surface. These can also be the most deadly.

- The most common reasons people postpone change are: fear, discouragement, rebellion, laziness, and procrastination.

- Admitting to your avoidance strategy is the first step to ushering change into your life.

Discussion Questions

1. Why do you think people avoid change?

2. Give an example of how you've avoided change in your life.

3. Of the five reasons identified as to why people most often avoid change, which one do you struggle with the most?

4. How does deciding to change impact your ability to overcome your tendency to avoid change?

5. If you asked your spouse or children to name something in your life that you needed to change, what do you think they would say?

Chapter 4

RECOGNIZE THAT CHANGE NEVER STOPS

The longer we avoid change, the more comfortable we grow with our struggles. Whatever limits us from living a life of abundance, passion, and satisfaction becomes normal and accepted the longer we wait to make the change. Over time, we lose the urgency or desire to change because we grow to like it.

One of my staff members said, "This is why I believe people don't change: because a known bondage is more comfortable than an unknown freedom." Did you catch that? A known bondage becomes more comfortable than an unknown freedom. That means we'd rather stay with the known bondage we have than consider thoughts of freedom to live life in all its fullness.

Have you ever asked yourself what's keeping you from changing? Maybe it's the thought of failure. Perhaps you've tried unsuccessfully to change in the past. Perhaps you've achieved change for a period of time but then fallen back into your old patterns. When we let past or present failure keep up from changing, we are choosing a known bondage rather than going and getting what God has for us.

What do you need to change? And don't let yourself off the hook by jumping to something obvious. Think deeper. Think bigger. What do you need to change spiritually, relationally, or emotionally? Who do you need to forgive? What has God been talking about to you? What has He convicted you about time and time again?

> A known bondage becomes more comfortable than an unknown freedom.

Today is your wake-up call. It's breakthrough time. It's time for you to change *before* you have to.

It's really easy to see the need to change in others, isn't it? You think, "Here's what that person needs to change. And here's what that other person needs to change. And there is someone else who needs to change, too." God wants you to point the finger at yourself. He wants you to take care of the log in your own eye before you go pointing out the speck in someone else's.

Now let me suggest a few areas I think need to change in your life. It might sound presumptuous for me to suggest these areas apply to everyone but hear me out on this. I think you'll find yourself in every one of these categories.

I will start with physical. I think we need to take care of our bodies. I've heard Christians say, "You know what? I'm going to Heaven, so I just don't care. I'll clog my arteries and get there quicker." I completely disagree. Your body is the temple of the Holy Spirit. You want to take care of it. You want to take care of what God gave you and do a good job with it.

I've heard people say, "Well, I'm staying in bed. I'm going to eat whatever I want. Make that a triple cheeseburger with mayo. Slather it on there. I just don't care." We keep saying whatever we need to because we haven't yet decided we want to change.

I remember watching a documentary about the life of actor Patrick Swayze, including an interview Barbara Walters had conducted with him. This particular show was aired just after he died from cancer. During the show, they highlighted how he battled for his life. I remember the conversation they showed with Patrick.

Someone asked him, "You've smoked for, like, forty years. Did you quit smoking now that you're battling cancer?" He said, "No." I have to admit that I lost a little compassion for him when he said that. Even while confronting death, he never regretted—nor stopped—smoking. Patrick Swayze refused to change, and it killed him.

I have seen this same thing with my own eyes. I've been at the hospital after a family member had a heart attack. His whole life has been turned upside down. Worse than that, I have been there talking to the widow—devastated at her husband's death, which might have been avoided had he decided to change. He wouldn't listen to what the doctor said or anyone else for that matter.

The doctors I talk to about this blatant disregard for truth are often amazed by the prevailing attitude among some of their patients. They tell me, "You know what we're amazed at? We tell people, you're going to die if you don't change. And they respond, 'Ah, you know, we're all gonna die some day.'" They are just amazed that people don't want to change. Personally, I think it's time for us to make physical changes

A second area is personal finances. Some of you need to change your financial situation. You need to start being a good steward with your money. You need to wake up and take care of what God's given you. You rant, "I don't want a budget! Budgets are evil! I can handle my money. I don't want a budget." Why not? Because it's painful. It's discipline. God is telling you it's time to change.

Maybe God is telling you to tithe, but you refuse. And you say, "God, I'll give you a little bit at the end of the week—whatever's left over. I'll give you a little something. Aren't you happy with that?"

And God says, "Why don't you honor Me with at least a tithe?"

And you say, "Well, you know, Lord, they'll still love me at my church if I don't tithe, so I'm okay." And you don't change.

The reason we don't change is because we live in a society that says, "Here's another credit card. Here's another opportunity. Here's another thing. Go ahead! Maybe *you'll* get a bail-out." I have news for you: It ain't gonna happen.

Some of us never make the financial changes we need to make. We just keep going down the same, destructive road. God wants you to change. You know you need to change. Maybe you've tried. For whatever reason, you're back in the same—or worse—financial situation. Don't give up! Change it, and never go back! (If you're serious about this, let me highly recommend Dave Ramsey's book *Financial Peace*.)

A third area many of us need to change is our relationships. Your marriage might be a total wreck, and you've never gone to a counselor. You might have a tenuous relationship with your children and aren't even on speaking terms. You might not have good relationships with your parents or siblings. Without a doubt, you need to experience change in this area of your life.

Let me speak to men for just a minute on a couple of things. First of all, the Bible says you're the priest of the home, the protector, and the provider (see Deut. 6:1–9; Ps. 127:41; 1 Cor. 11:3; and Eph. 6:4, 25–29). Everything that comes into the home comes through you. You're the leader. And if your marriage is not right, you're the one who is supposed to take the lead to fix it. Don't wait until your wife comes to you and says, "Honey, could we go to counseling?" *You* should be proactive. *You* should be the leader of your family.

I've seen so many marriages that are a wreck because of poor decisions that lead to silent addictions. The primary example is pornography. It starts small, and technology makes it so convenient.

Some of you reading this are in the middle of this addiction, and you've toyed around with pornography long enough to get hooked. You come home, sit in front of the computer, and pornography has become your release. As a result, you've neglected your marriage. You've neglected what you're supposed to do, and you've become addicted to this. And you know you should change.

You've thought about changing but nothing has really changed in your life. I have to ask: How serious are you? Are you going to continue to play the game? Are you going to put a filter on your computer? Are you going to have an accountability partner?

Don't just go halfway. God's not happy with that. He says, "Will you change before you have to, or are you going to get busted at work, get fired, and have to tell your wife why you got fired?" Worse—are you going to get busted at home when your kid pops into the home office to ask you a question about his homework only to catch you viewing something you should not be viewing? It's easier to change before you have to. And so I'm challenging you: If you are there, it's time to change before you have to. God wants you to change.

The final area for change that I want to identify is your spiritual condition. God may be telling you to make changes in this area of your life. If so, you need to change.

Here's what happens to a lot of people in church, perhaps even to you. You give your heart to Jesus. You become an authentic follower of Jesus. And dramatic change takes place. I mean, it's dramatic change.

You announce, "Okay. No more of this sin or that failure. God does not want me to do that. I am going to stop that." And then you say, "Okay, God does not want me to get drunk, smoke pot" . . . or whatever it is you're doing that you know you need to change. You commit to stopping it. And all of a sudden you take it to the next level. You decide God no longer wants you to use profanity. And so you start changing. You experience dramatic change in your life because you give your heart to Jesus.

But then there's a thing that creeps into your life—casual commitment. You get comfortable and "settle in" to your Christian faith. You've got the rough edges smoothed out. People would never hear profanity come out of your mouth. You would never talk about being drunk, or actually be drunk. You never commit the "big" sins, but all of a sudden you've grown comfortable and casual in your commitment to Christ. As a result, you stop changing.

If you've been following Christ for a while and you're not changing, you're in trouble. Because complacency has set in, and you know what happens then? There's always a current working against you.

> If you are not moving towards Him, you are moving away from Him.

Did you know that? There is a spiritual current working on you to pull you away from God. If you are not moving towards Him, you are moving away from Him. You may not even know you're drifting. Before you know it, you'll find yourself in your pastor's office saying, "It just came out of nowhere. I gave in to that sin, and I didn't want to. It just sneaked up on me. I should've known better! I've been following the Lord for twenty-five years. I should've known better!"

So God says, "Change! And never stop changing." I want to be more like Jesus next year than I am this year. I want to be closer to Him. I want another challenge. I want another obstacle to overcome.

I remember when I started River Valley Church with only thirteen people. Every day was a step of faith. I didn't realize this when I was in the middle of it, but it's become clear to me looking back.

I remember praying, "God, if the offering isn't at least this much, I can't even pay the staff. God, please make this work." I remember worrying if anyone would show up. I still remember signing the lease to one of our current buildings and realizing we were risking it all to make this step of faith.

And I remember complaining, "God, when does it stop? When does it get easy?"

And He said, "It never stops. If you want to be where I want you to be, it will never stop."

In that moment I resolved, "All right, well, at least I know where we're going now. We're never going to stop. This is a journey of change."

Hear that word today. If you have stopped changing, you are in trouble. You are likely in a dangerous drift. You are in danger of getting into big trouble.

CHAPTER 4 IN REVIEW

Key Ideas

- A known bondage is more comfortable than an unknown freedom.

- It's easier sometimes to see the need for others to change before we recognize the need to change in our own lives.

- Areas in our lives we might need to change include physical/ health, financial, relationships, and spiritual.

- If you've been following Christ for a while and you're not changing, you're in trouble. There is a spiritual current working on you to pull you away from God.

- Never stop changing.

Discussion Questions

1. When do you think a person resisting change becomes aware that they are resisting change?

2. Why is it harder to change the longer you take to begin making changes?

3. Name at least one area that has required ongoing changes in or adjustments to your life. Describe your journey in this area.

4. What role does casual commitment play in delaying the change process?

5. Is there something in your life that is causing you to drift away from your faith? If so, what?

Chapter 5

BELIEVE CHANGE
IS POSSIBLE

We've discussed some really deep stuff, but we're just getting started. This first section is about preparing to change. We've talked about the need for change, how we play at change, what we do to resist or avoid change, and why change never stops. In the last part of this section, I want to make sure you don't miss this truth: Change is possible in your life if you believe you can change.

Let me give you the good news. God has given you the power to change. He's been giving us the power to change from the beginning. In Philippians 2:13, Paul says, "For it is God who works in you to will and to act according to his good purpose." What an important truth for you and I to consider.

God is working in you. He is working in you right now, and He's giving you the power to make the change. So don't live with excuses. He's given you the power to change and to say, "I can do this. I can make it. It's time for me to change."

An important part of creating personal change is your belief that change is possible. If you can't visualize life after the change, you're highly unlikely to be able to make the change. I'm not trying to be a downer. I just understand the power personal belief plays in our ability to change the circumstances in our lives. It's a fundamental reality. You are not a victim but an empowered being who has the capacity to accept a life of abundance, passion, and satisfaction.

There is a really great prayer I want you to know about. It's a very popular one. I was shocked when I realized I was only familiar with the first part. The last half—the part I had never heard before—contained something I didn't expect. This whole prayer is very meaningful to me, and I know it has been for so many others.

Below is the full text of a variation of "The Serenity Prayer" written by Reinhold Niebuhr:

> God, grant me the serenity
> to accept the things I cannot change,
> the courage to change the things I can,
> and the wisdom to know the difference.
> Living one day at a time,
> enjoying one moment at a time;
> accepting hardship as a pathway to peace;
> taking, as Jesus did,
> this sinful world as it is,
> not as I would have it;
> trusting that You will make all things right
> if I surrender to Your will;
> so that I may be reasonably happy in this life
> and supremely happy with You forever in the next.
> Amen.

If you're like most people, that's the first time you've read the entire Serenity prayer. Pretty good stuff, don't you think? I want to ask you to do something that might feel strange. I want you to re-read the prayer above out loud. It might even help to say it to someone. There is power that comes in speaking something versus simply thinking it. Communication experts generally agree that an idea, thought, feeling, or emotion isn't real or tangible until it is expressed aloud—however well or poorly delivered. I would agree.

Start reading right now. Say the prayer out loud to yourself or someone you love and trust. Think about the words you are speaking as you read through this prayer.

I learned this prayer at our Celebrate Recovery ministry. I started this ministry in my church. God told me to start Celebrate Recovery, and I had never ever been drunk in my life. I've never tried drugs, and

> My hope is that you will change before you have to and not because you have to.

yet God said, "Here you go. Start Celebrate Recovery." (Maybe it was Little Debbie snack cakes, and I missed it all these years! Oops!) Nevertheless, it's powerful.

Celebrate Recovery is a ministry that began at Saddleback Church in Southern California more than twenty years ago. It's for serious, life-controlling addictions that are out there. And we pray "The Serenity Prayer" every time we get together. Even if you're not part of Celebrate Recovery or even think you struggle with any addictions, this prayer will encourage you to reach for a deeper life experience than you have today.

When we talk about personal life change, we tend to evaluate our own lives through rose-colored glasses. We dismiss the things we know we need to change because we're not addicted to drugs, alcohol, or sex. Let me tell you something: Addiction is addiction. It's doesn't matter if it's to methamphetamine or to work. It's all the same in God's eyes. Anything that takes our attention away from Him and steals our joy and abundant life is wrong and should be changed.

There is at least one thing in your life you need to change. You may have a lot of reasons for not making any changes in one or more areas of your life. I bet that one of them is that you lack the belief that change is really possible. If that's you, my encouragement to you is to keep pressing forward. Don't give up! Keep fighting! Sometimes our belief—in ourselves and in God—grows stronger when we are stretched beyond what we think we can endure or accomplish.

My prayer for you is that you will experience the power within you to change because God's Word is true. My prayer is that you will know the things you can't change and the things that you can. With that knowledge, my hope is that you will change. More importantly, my hope is that you will change before you have to and not because you have to.

CHAPTER 5 IN REVIEW

Key Ideas

+ God has given you the power to change.

+ God is working in you right now, and He's giving you the power to make the change.

+ An important part of creating personal change is your belief that change is possible.

+ If you can't visualize life after the change, you're highly unlikely to be able to make the change.

+ Sometimes our belief—in ourselves and in God—grows stronger when we are stretched beyond what we think we can endure or accomplish.

Discussion Questions

1. What about change seems the most impossible to you?

2. List three things you learned about change by reading "The Serenity Prayer."

3. Does it make "The Serenity Prayer" any more personal for you when you read it out loud instead of just reading it on the page? If so, how?

4. Why does our faith grow stronger by being stretched? Describe a time in your life when this happened.

5. Do you believe you can change? Why? Why not?

SECTION
TWO

FOLLOW
THE PATH TO
CHANGE

Chapter 6

BUILD
ON YOUR PAST

'll tell you what's really frustrating as a pastor is waiting on people to change. You keep telling them the truth. You keep preaching the truth. Maybe you counsel with people again and again and again. But they never change.

No matter how much I want them to change, until they decide to change, nothing lasting takes place. Years can go by—maybe five, six, seven, or even ten years—and they're still doing the same things they were doing before. These people are trapped in their past mistakes, hurts, habits, and hang-ups. They never seem to be able to break free.

Now I don't know anybody who thinks this situation describes his or her situation. Not a one. The paradox is that people who refuse to make changes in their lives are bound to replay the same loop in life until they decide to change.

We tell ourselves that we are all good when we're not. I have to confess this is very frustrating as a pastor. I want to help people make positive changes in their lives. I want people to grow and become more like God.

45

But some never change. How unfortunate!

I'm writing this book for you—and for that person. I'm a relentless optimist. I believe that persistence is the human expression of God's patience. If God's not going to give up on you, then I'm not either.

A lot of us don't change before we have to. A lot of us refuse to change until the pain of not changing exceeds the pain of changing. This is also affectionately known as the School of Hard Knocks.

You know what I'm talking about. We keep doing the same things and running into the same wall and wondering why we don't see different results. We throw up our hands in defeat and resolve in our minds that change is impossible. Not true! I want you to know that change is possible. You can make the change you need to make. You just have to let go of your past.

> Persistence is the human expression of God's patience.

A few people make change seem easy. You know who I'm talking about. You could probably say their names right now. They make change seem so easy, they make your stomach turn.

When we encounter those people, we often excuse ourselves from changing because we could never do what they did in their lives. We could never repair our marriage, improve our relationship with our children, secure that job promotion, get out of debt, or finally lose those extra pounds we've been carrying around. We tell ourselves that we're not smart enough, good enough, or disciplined enough. But that's not true.

The biggest obstacle people endure to making a change in their lives is living in their past. You can't change what happened yesterday. Sometimes our poor decisions created the situations and circumstances we find ourselves in today. But the good news is that if our decisions put us in our negative position today, our decisions can also change our circumstances for good.

Your past will either trap you, or it will propel you forward. It will either hold you back or force you to move forward. You are not your past. Today is the day you can make a change and begin working toward a different life—one of abundance, passion, and satisfaction.

Most of us try to make the change and follow through. When we do, the world seems to come against us. Has that ever happened to you? It happens to me, too. You declare that today you are going to start a diet. Of course, as soon as you decide, all you can find in your pantry is a Ding Dong.

Or even better, you go to the door in the middle of the afternoon. It's the neighbor you haven't talked to in ten years. You wonder why she is at your door in the middle of the afternoon. When you open the door, she explains that she was baking pies today and decided to make an extra one for you. You have to say "thank you" and bring the pie into your house. And you have to eat a piece because you know she is going to ask you what you thought about it. Wow! Am I the only one that happens to? I hope not!

I talked to a guy who told me as soon as he decided to make a change, his world started to feel like it was coming apart. I think his exact words were, "The wheels fell off." But he went on to explain that he just moved forward in spite of that because he had decided to push through the change he had been avoiding for so long.

You will face plenty of obstacles when you decide to make a change. It's going to happen. You might as well expect them and get ready for them.

We're going to talk about this more specifically in a later section of this book. Right now I want to focus on people who have the ability to change before they have to. There are people who don't have to go to the School of Hard Knocks. There's just something in them. They have an ability that allows them to say, "I don't have to go through the pain in order to do the right thing." It's very rare, but that attitude is possible.

Most of us, though, need pain before we will change. Do you realize that? Most of us need pain in order to change. We need a crisis, a tragedy, a catastrophe, or something that happens that we don't like. When that happens, it forces us to change.

You may say, "Pastor Rob, I come from a bad family. I can't overcome it. Pastor Rob, there are things in my life that I can't change. I don't have the ability to change because, after all, this is what happened to me, this is what is in my life, this is my family, and this is my story. No one in my family ever changes. It's just the way things are." Let me tell you something: you can change if you choose to. The question is when; will it be before you have to or because you have to?

Sometimes the pain in our past gives us the strength to make the change we need to make for our future. Paul wrote in Romans 8:28, "And we know that in all things God works for the good of those who love him, who have been called according to his purpose." You can use your past to create the change you need in your life because God has already made it possible to turn bad things into good, to take trash and make it a treasure, and to give you a second chance even when you don't think you deserve it.

> Most of us need pain in order to change.

Don't let your past keep you from changing. Decide to change, and use your past as a building block for future success. This is possible for you because it's what God intended from the beginning.

CHAPTER 6 IN REVIEW

Key Ideas

- No matter how much someone else wants you to change, you can't change until you make the decision to change.

- People who refuse to change are trapped by their past mistakes, hurts, habits, and hang-ups.

- A lot of people refuse to change until the pain of not changing exceeds the pain of changing.

- The biggest obstacle people endure to making a change in their lives is living in their past.

- The pain of our past often gives us the strength to make the change we need to for the future.

Discussion Questions

1. List three changes you have delayed making in your life. Why?

2. How does your past influence your future?

3. Describe a painful event or experience in your past that makes you think change is impossible in a particular area of your life.

4. Is there someone you need to forgive or an offense you need to let go of before you can start making a change in your life? Consider doing this in person or over the phone in the next twenty-four hours.

5. Identify someone in your life who used their painful past to create a significant future. How did they find the courage to make the change? If you don't know, try reaching out to that person over lunch, dinner, or coffee to learn from their success.

Chapter 7

TRY NEW WAYS OF DOING FAMILIAR THINGS

When I was young, new and different was cool. It was a badge of honor to break out of the pack and do things in a way that was different from everyone else. The older I get the more I like things to stay the way they are. Thus, the idea of change or learning new ways to do familiar things becomes a little less appealing. That doesn't remove the fact that we were created to change and adapt—constantly. The only time we are fully free of change is when we're dead. Until then, living life to the fullest—that is with abundance, passion, and satisfaction—means change must always be in the mix.

I want to tell you about two people who chose to adapt and change even though they didn't know what that change would mean for them in the beginning. I think that's where a lot of us are today. We often know we need to change, but we're not sure we're ready to give up what's familiar for the great unknown. We can learn a lot from these two.

Daniel is one of my favorite people in the Bible (Old Testament). Nothing seemed to distract him from his commitment to and personal convictions about change—even if it put his life in danger. I don't know many people who would be willing to risk death to practice their faith. This guy is all in, for sure.

Now I want to clarify that when we talk about people in the Bible doing amazing things, I want to be careful that I don't paint an unrealistic, super-human person for you. Even though the Bible uses an economy of words to deliver only the most significant and important details, Daniel was a human being just like you and me. And his life was anything but ordinary—just in case you feared that he had it easy or something.

In the ancient world, battles between nations were not uncommon. Diplomacy hadn't exactly been created yet. When the nation-state of Israel was first divided and later conquered, the conquering party—in this case, the Babylonians—separated the best and brightest and brought them back as spoils of war. They became part of their culture. This was a big deal because it meant that Daniel was separated from all things familiar— customs, geography, and especially family.

Daniel and his captive peers were expected to adopt the culture of the Babylonians. You might be wondering what the big deal is all about. God gave the Israelites specific rules about what they could and could not eat. The Babylonians did not follow these same rules and were not going to facilitate the rules of the captive Israelites. This made Daniel's decision to request an alternate, Israelite dinner plan surprising and unprecedented. It was a dangerous decision because there were no laws protecting peoples' preferences in Babylon like there are in America today.

Daniel didn't want to eat the Babylonian food because he knew that wasn't right. Before taking one bite of the Babylonian king's food—and even before he got overweight and lazy and had high cholesterol and all the things that often come before we decide to change—he requested an alternate meal plan that was consistent with Jewish traditions and laws. The only problem was that the Babylonians really didn't care much about Jewish anything. They had just conquered this nation, after all.

So Daniel decided that he wanted to make a change before he had to. He stood up and said, "I'd like permission to eat this diet and not that one." Daniel made the decision to stay true to himself and what he believed was the best option—even in an unfortunate and potentially dangerous situation. Daniel had something within him that enabled him to make the change no matter the cost.

Introducing change into our lives means we have to be open to new things. It means leaving something behind in order to take on something different. Change causes us to establish a new normal that is very often in stark contrast to what is familiar and comfortable to us right now.

> Introducing change into our lives means we have to be open to new things.

This was certainly true for Daniel. He was in a new place, surrounded by a completely different culture. His captors asked him to do things that were unusual and out of the ordinary. The important thing is that in the middle of the change, Daniel never compromised his core convictions. The same is true for us. In the midst of change, we have to have something we can hold on to in order to give us the confidence to move forward. Daniel adapted to his new surroundings and his new lifestyle but he never compromised what he believed was truth. The key here is that he "purposed in his heart" that he would not defile himself. This is what Daniel 1:8 says. (Other translations say, "he was determined," "he resolved not to," "he made up his mind.")

Here's the deal. When your heart truly belongs to God you can go anywhere and face any situation and you'll be okay because you are determined to do the right thing.

Being open to new ways of doing familiar things means we recognize that change will bring about new patterns and habits. It also means that we will have to give up our preferences for a greater outcome. However, no change that asks you to change or compromise God's truth is the kind of change you want to make.

Now there's another guy in the Bible who had the same kind of commitment to change that Daniel had. He wanted change. He did it before he was confronted. Now eventually he was confronted, but he was on his way to changing.

We read about Zacchaeus in the New Testament. I think we've dogged that guy—a lot. You know who Zacchaeus was: he was the "wee little man," right? And we sing that song about him climbing up a sycamore tree. Honestly, I feel sorry for the guy. How would you like it if similar songs were written about you?

Those of you who have grown up in church are singing the song right now, getting to the spot where you sing, "Zacchaeus, you come down!" while wagging your finger at him. But nothing was going to keep Zacchaeus from what he wanted. Here's a guy who was excited that Jesus was coming through his town. He thought, "I've heard about this guy. I need something in my life. What do I need? I want to go see Jesus; I want to be around him. I've got to get a look at him. I'm a short guy, and I can't see. I'm climbing the tree. I have to get a look. I have to get close. I just have to see this guy." And I love that he was making the change before he had to. Here's what the Bible says happened. Zacchaeus volunteered to give away his money, pay back debts, and he did this even before Jesus really talked with him! He was changing before he had to! Now, eventually Jesus had a conversation with him and explained what he had to do to radically change his life, but I love that he was going after change even before he knew that Jesus would personally address him.

Both Daniel and Zacchaeus probably felt awkward about the changes they made, but they didn't let that hold them back. It didn't matter to them what other people thought; it didn't matter what difficulties they might experience. The change needed to take place, and they both resolved to make it happen—even though they didn't completely understand how it would happen.

How many of us never change because we're not willing to look stupid? We fear that other people won't understand our need to change and will disagree with our decision. Really, we fear that they won't like us anymore if we change. We may even wonder if we'll like ourselves after the change.

Such thoughts, questions, and fears are normal. Anytime we try new things, it feels awkward. Whether it's a first kiss, first solo car drive, or first night of marriage, new things are just awkward. That's okay. It's not a reason not to make the change. It just means that change requires us to form a new normal.

Addiction recovery programs often talk about "faking it until you make it." It's solid advice in my opinion. Those who have overcome addictions understand that forming new habits takes time and repetition. But it begins with a strong desire to exchange familiar habits and responses to life's situations and circumstances for new ones. In the midst of that, you *get* it. It becomes clear. And what is familiar—like fear, stress, and regret—is dealt with in new ways. This is when you know that true, authentic change has taken place in your life. It really is one of the keys to changing before you have to.

Maybe there is some change you've wanted to make in your life that seems impossible. Maybe it's change that is simply adjusting your response to normal, everyday feelings and experiences. Whatever change you want to make, it begins with letting go of the familiar and choosing to respond in new ways. Internally there's a purpose in your heart, a desperate desire to change. Without a commitment to new things, your change won't last.

CHAPTER 7 IN REVIEW

Key Ideas

- Living life to the fullest—that is with abundance, passion, and satisfaction—means change must always be in the mix.

- We often know we need to change, but we're not sure we're ready to give up what's familiar for the great unknown.

- Introducing change into our lives means we have to be open to new things.

- Change causes us to establish a new normal that is very often in stark contrast to what is familiar and comfortable to us right now.

- Whatever change you want to make, it begins with letting go of the familiar and choosing to respond in new ways.

Discussion Questions

1. Why does change seem easier when we are younger? Why does change seem more difficult as we get older?

2. If you were Daniel, would you have made the same decision he did? Why? Why not?

3. What change are you holding out on because you fear looking stupid to other people?

4. Name one change that you don't feel you have the courage to make. What step(s) can you take today toward making that change in your life?

5. Think about a time in your life when you "faked it until you made it." How did your actions influence your feelings over time?

Chapter 8

DECIDE TO BE
A PERSON OF ACTION

The shortest distance between two points is a straight line. Even though we know this is mathematically true, it is also true in our personal lives. A straight line represents action—leaving behind one point in time as you move toward a new destination. The reason you're not seeing anything different take place in your life is because you're not taking action; you're not leaving behind what's holding you back. Here's the guy who I believe will deliver the insight we need to not be held back but to change before we have to. His name is Josiah.

Josiah became King of Israel very early in life—he was eight years old (see 2 Kings 22:1). I know some kids that age who think they are king. This guy was the real deal.

His dad was not considered such a great king. He didn't follow God's laws, and he allowed a lot of not-so-good things to take place. Josiah would eventually repair the damage caused by his father's unfortunate decisions and give us the keys to change.

Josiah's desire to live for God was the right thing to do. One of his most important decisions was to raise money to repair and restore the temple—where God's people worshipped. The temple was in disrepair. He knew it needed to be cleaned up and put back together again. Josiah believed that fixing up the temple would help his people come back to their faith and follow God again.

While the reconstruction was underway, someone discovered a scroll. They discovered part of the Bible, but not just any book of the Bible. It was one of the first five books of the Bible—the Torah. For Josiah and his people it was a really big deal. Very likely the scroll had been hidden by one of the evil kings before him because people with bad intentions don't want to hear truth. Don't you agree? I know when I'm not doing what I should do I really don't want to hear someone else tell me that it's not right.

The workers who found the scroll brought it to Josiah and asked what to do with it. Josiah was curious, so he decided to read it. Makes sense to me. Why not?

If I want to know what God wants, it only makes sense to browse His instruction book, the Bible. Someone in love with God, who had a heart for the things of God, would want to read it, too. Josiah saw no other option but to check it out.

So they read it to him, and they read how they should be living as the people of God. He realized he had been living right as the king, but his people were not living right. He said, "I'm living right. I'm doing the right things. I'm walking with God. I'm not turning to the left or the right, but my country is not living right."

In 2 Kings 22, the Bible says, "When the king heard the words of the Book of the Law, he tore his robes. He gave these orders to Hilkiah the priest, Ahikam son of Shaphan, Acbor son of Micaiah." (It goes without saying that you should know better than to name your kids these names, right? I hope so.) Josiah said:

> Go and inquire of the LORD for me and for the people and for all
> Judah about what is written in this book that has been found. Great
> is the LORD's anger that burns against us because our fathers have

not obeyed the words of this book; they have not acted in accordance with all that is written there concerning us (2 Kings 22:11–13).

Now the first thing that strikes me about this is that Josiah heard God's truth and responded with humility. The guy tore his clothes. This was a sign of great grief. This was a way of saying, "I'm sorry, God. I've been the leader of these people, and You know my heart has been for You. But these people aren't doing right." He tore his clothes in sorrow and he humbled himself.

Josiah shows us that if we're going to be people who change before we have to, we need humility. Now, the world says have pride. Be proud of yourself. Have pride, advance, and be strong. Don't be humble. Humble people sit in the back. You don't want that. You want to be proud. (Remember Pharaoh—pride kills!)

But Josiah said, "You know what? I'm in great grief. I don't have it figured out. When confronted with God's truth, I'm humble and willing to say we need to make more change because I don't want to go any farther in this disaster. I don't want to have these bad things happen and all this judgment, because I'm humble before You, God."

Do you know that we're a prideful people? We do what we want to do because that's what sinful hearts do. We convince ourselves that we have the right to live our lives however we want to. What prideful attitudes!

Doctors are shocked by this blatant obsession with personal needs, wants, and desires to the point that there is no regard for truth. I know when I talked to my doctor about changing before I had to, he told me that he rarely encountered someone so interested in making a change before he had to. I said, "This is my cholesterol, and this has to change."

He said, "That's great that you're doing this. You know, most people I tell that their cholesterol is high and they're going to die if they don't make a change look at me like I'm an idiot." It's really a sad commentary on a culture that claims to be so advanced in so many ways. It's hard to label yourself advanced if you miss the basics.

Pride gives us the false confidence that we know best. It doesn't matter that your doctor went to medical school, he or she is immediately wrong. It doesn't matter that you have no idea what you're talking about because your sister or mother has figured it out for you. What's up with that?

The medical community has a word for this; it is *noncompliance*. This happens when the doctor gives his patient some medicine, tells the patient what to do, and yet the patient doesn't do it because he thinks he knows better than the doctor. I mean after all, I didn't go to medical school, did you? Because I know that I don't know, I'm going to listen to what my doctor says.

I've always been a good patient. Even when I faced major surgery at the age of eleven for a caved in chest, I did everything the doctor told me to do. I guess that made it easy for me to take very specific notes while the doctor was telling me about the things I needed to consider while trying to lose weight. I took those notes and followed them without question because I'm confident he knows more than I do. What other appropriate response is there?

But we're so prideful. If we're going to be people who are willing to change before we have to—listen, this is key—we're going to have to be humble people who say, "God, You know more than I do. Tell me what I need to do, and I'll do it."

When God speaks to us about the changes we need to make in our lives, it's not a suggestion. God's voice brings instructions, not suggestions. It's not our place to argue. Are you really going to argue with the One who created you? Seriously?

> God's voice brings instructions, not suggestions.

But the reality is, we do it all the time. We say, "Thanks for the suggestion! Appreciate it. I'll take it under careful consideration and get back with You." What a destructive attitude that is.

We can't claim God as Lord and not do what He says. Yet that's the way we live. Why? Because we're prideful. If we're going to change before we have to, that means we don't need a tragedy to take place before we change. We need to expose ourselves to God's truth and—like Josiah—decide to bring our lives in line with that truth.

Doing that takes a lot of humility. The Bible says, "God opposes the proud but gives grace to the humble" (James 4:6). Humility means becoming a person of action—action based on God's truth, not on our truth. The Bible says we should "grieve, mourn, and wail. . . . Humble yourselves before the Lord, and he will lift you up" (James 4:9–10).

If we're going to be people who will change before we have to, we have to admit that we don't have the answers to life all figured out. God has not given us all the wisdom of the world, and there are smarter people than us out there. We serve under people in authority who want to help us grow; yet our own pride, our lack of humility keeps us from growing.

A humble heart is the key to change. How many times have you discovered that pride does not give you a happy ending? I'm sure you've heard this saying many times in your life: "Pride goeth before the fall." You've got to have humility. (Even Disney kids' movies know this!)

If you're reading this and you're not "that religious," this still applies to you! There are experts who can speak into your life and save you lots of grief and pain, but you have to listen to them. Humble yourself and make the changes you need to make. If that's you, maybe this is the moment you humble yourself and say, "I don't have all the answers, so I'll listen and respond to the voice that's telling me to change." Your whole eternity hangs in the balance. Humble yourself and listen to the voice of change.

When humility replaces pride in our lives, then we'll be ready to become a person of action. People who only talk about change never really change. It's a prideful way of ignoring what we know to be true about ourselves.

If we will ever get over ourselves and our need to be right, we'll find that humility—not pride—leads to the life of abundance, passion, and satisfaction that we so desperately are looking for. Until humility replaces pride and leads to action, it will be nearly impossible to leave behind what's holding us back. We simultaneously try to convince ourselves that we can put off the change instead of becoming someone who changes before we have to.

CHAPTER 8 IN REVIEW

Key Ideas

- The reason you're not seeing anything different take place in your life is because you're not taking action; you never left behind what's holding you back.

- If I want to know what God wants, it only makes sense to seek His instruction.

- Pride gives us the false confidence that we know best, but a humble heart is the first key to changing before we have to.

- When God speaks to us about the change we need to make in our lives, it's not a suggestion.

- People who talk about change never really change. It's a prideful way of ignoring what we know to be true about ourselves.

Discussion Questions

1. Why is action such an easy concept to grasp but a difficult one to practice?

2. How does pride prevent us from taking action?

3. Is humility a trait that is valued in society? Why? Why not?

4. What areas of your life are living "noncompliant" to God's instruction?

5. Have you been talking about change instead of taking action and actually making change?

Chapter 9

RESPOND TO
WHAT IS TRUE

Once we decide to become people who take action—to change before we have to—it brings us to another important juncture. That is, action forces us to determine what we believe is truth and what we believe isn't. Taking action in and of itself isn't enough. We have to understand the actions we take within the context of what we know to be truth.

Let's continue with the story of Josiah. When he realized that his people were not living consistent with God's truth, his humility lead him to tear his clothes. Now let me caution you. I don't want you going around tearing your clothes. And I think it goes without saying that I don't want you to tear anyone else's clothes either. That's another book. Not this one. Sorry.

In the ancient world, tearing your clothes was a way of outwardly expressing your inward pain. Josiah felt so much regret and pain that his people were not following God's truth that he had to find a way to express it. What he did next was precisely because his actions were based on truth—not his own personal idea of truth, but God's truth.

He immediately went to work. This is another key to change! Don't procrastinate! Josiah decided to respond to God's truth and acted to bring change instead of waiting for a tragedy to bring change. When we respond to what we know is God's truth, we have the strength to make the change today. Too often, though, we put it off until tomorrow. If that's you, it's precisely because you are not responding to the truth of God that you know.

Most of us know when we don't have a heart that is right before God. We keep telling ourselves, "Tomorrow I will get right with God." Tomorrow. Yet tomorrow doesn't come. I want you to change right now. Take action. Respond to the God's truth today.

Josiah took action. He aligned the actions and behavior of his country with what he read in God's Word. He confronted people who were living inconsistently with God's truth and told them to stop. Josiah didn't do it just once; he did it again and again until the people followed him and—most importantly—remembered what God had said about the way they should live, the things they should value, and who they should worship (see 2 Kings 23).

It took guts to do that because he had to take away what the people loved, what they had grown comfortable with. They were attached—maybe addicted—to those things, but Josiah said, "No more! This is not pleasing to God." It was time for the people to respond to God's truth.

Josiah determined his people were going to do the right thing. He was a man of action, so he restored the Passover. He cleaned God's house and said, "This is the way we're going to live." That guy was a man of action. He was convicted. He didn't just say, "Oh, that's good for me. I'll just keep it quiet with me." He said, "It's good for everybody."

This leads me to the third key in Josiah's life. He had a responsive heart. Before we can change, we have to be people of action who get off the fence and make the hard decisions. We have to respond in a way that is consistent with God's truth because truth isn't relative; it's specific and universal. Talk is cheap. We say, "Oh, I'll change. I'm going to change." But we never do the hard stuff. Listen to what God says about this:

Because your heart was responsive and you humbled yourself before the LORD when you heard what I have spoken against this place and its people, that they would become accursed and laid waste, and because you tore your robes and wept in my presence, I have heard you, declares the LORD. Therefore I will gather you to your fathers, and you will be buried in peace. Your eyes will not see all the disaster I am going to bring on this place (2 Kings 22:19).

We have to have a responsive heart. The Bible says, "Because your heart was responsive." I think that if we're going to be people who change before we have to, we have to have responsive hearts—hearts that say, "You know what? I'm confronted with truth, and I respond to it. I'm open to it."

I think this is key. Don't miss this. Humility, action, and responsiveness work together to empower us to make the tough decisions, get off the fence, and make the changes in our lives that we know we need to make.

> Truth isn't relative; it's specific and universal.

We must have a heart that says, "God, I'll do what You say. I want to do what You say. I don't just hear it and debate it. I have a responsive, ready to go heart, and when You tell me what to do, I do it." Now, I believe God has allowed me to develop a responsive heart, and I believe my parents played a really key part in this.

When I was a kid in junior high, I wanted to see a movie that I knew I shouldn't go see. Even though I knew that I shouldn't see it, all my friends were going to see it. This moment has stuck on my life, and I've shared it many times before because I believe it was a moment where my parents helped me to develop a responsive heart. They said, "Why don't you go down to your room and just pray and ask God if you should go to the movie?" I didn't think that was fair, but I decided to see what I could find out.

So I went to my room and prayed, "Okay, God, You know this movie all my friends are going to see it. Can I go see it, too?"

Honestly, I just felt like God said, "You can't see it." It wasn't an audible voice but just a whisper that I heard. Now, I had a moment there to either have a responsive heart or a hard heart toward God. I want you to know, my family wasn't against all movies; they were against harmful movies. That's a big difference. So this was a real test for me and I needed to pass it.

In that moment I decided that God was right. I could have told my parents two things: "It's not the right thing to do," which would have led to a responsive heart; or I could have said "God's cool with it," which would have led to a hardened heart. I knew how God wanted me to respond. (Remember Pharaoh? A hardened heart didn't work for him, so I knew it wouldn't work for me!)

> If we're going to be people who change before we have to, we have to have responsive hearts.

We still laugh about it, but I still struggle with this sometimes. God's Word confronts us with truth, yet we try to convince ourselves that God is comfortable with the things we want to do that we know He does not want us to do. After all, God wants us to be happy, right? And whatever it is, I'm happier as a result of it.

But God says, "I didn't say that. Doing this thing will hurt you. You don't understand it now, but you will." God is not comfortable with your sin or bad habits just because you are comfortable with them. Don't confuse the two. Too often, we convince ourselves that it's okay while God says no, it's not.

Do you know the Holy Spirit will lead you into all truth? (See John 16:13.) The Holy Spirit will convict you of the things you're doing wrong. When that happens, you have an opportunity. You can either have a responsive heart or a hard heart. The more you ignore the voice of God, the more you start pushing Him away and stiff-arming God, the more your heart gets hardened and the more difficult it becomes to respond to God. God wants us to have a responsive heart.

Now, when I got up from praying about that movie and went up to my mom and dad, I told them God said no. I said, "He said no, and I need to obey Him."

They said, "We knew God was going to say no. We didn't know how you'd respond. We didn't know if you'd have a responsive heart or not and we're glad that we're seeing that God is building a responsive heart in you."

We need to be able to say to God and other voices of wisdom, "I will have a responsive heart; I'll be humble before you." We need to take action when He tells us things. And when the truth of His Word convicts us, we need to respond in a way that is consistent with His truth.

Commit to respond to God right now—even if you've been holding out. Resolve to do the right thing before the wrong thing takes place. And keep that responsive heart. Just stay responsive, and you'll discover your life will be filled with abundance, passion, and satisfaction.

CHAPTER 9 IN REVIEW

Key Ideas

- ◆ When we respond to what we know is truth, we have the strength to make the change today.

- ◆ We've have to be humble before we can really learn what truth is.

- ◆ God is not comfortable with your sin just because you are comfortable with it.

- ◆ The more you ignore the voice of God, the more you start pushing Him away and stiff-arming God, the more your heart gets hardened, the more difficult it becomes to respond to God.

- ◆ Humility, action, and responsiveness work together to empower us to make the tough decisions, get off the fence, and make the change in our lives that we know we need to make.

Discussion Questions

1. How does truth inform how we will respond?

2. Why do humility and a commitment to action come before our actual response? If we don't have humility or a commitment to action, how likely it is that we will respond?

3. Why does refusing to change become easier and more comfortable to live with over time?

4. Give an example of how your parents helped you have a responsive heart. If you're a parent, give an example of how you're helping your children develop responsive hearts.

5. What checkpoints can we place in our lives to make sure we keep responsive hearts?

Chapter 10

ALIGN YOUR FAITH
WITH YOUR DECISIONS

Now as I close this section of the book, let me just tell you this. The most significant thing you can do to prepare for change is to check your life's alignment. What are you measuring your life against? Is it the expectations of others? Is it a past you can't seem to escape?

When the tires on my car aren't in alignment with each other, the car doesn't drive well. In fact, if I don't do anything about it, it will eventually cause some significant damage. The reason we put our tires in alignment with each other is because the focus needs to be on getting where we need to go, not wondering if what we're driving is going to get us there safely.

Our lives aren't much different. When our values—or faith—is out of line with our decisions, we can do significant damage to our lives before we realize it. Our experience is different, however, when our decisions are in alignment with our faith in God. Just like our cars, if we don't make a change, it could harm us. This is why we need to change before we have to instead of because we have to.

When our two boys were younger, I started asking them this series of questions when I put them to bed: "How's your heart? How's your spirit? Are we good?" I don't know if you do that as a parent, but I still do. (Of course, now that they're teenagers they often put me to bed long before they go to bed themselves.)

If your kids are like mine, you can't just ask them one time and expect them to give you an honest answer. I have to ask them ten times. Usually around the last two or three times I ask them, they hear what I'm asking and respond with a nugget of honesty.

I want to ask you right now: How's your heart? How's your spirit? Are we good? If you're still reading, I guess I haven't pushed you over the edge yet. If you're hanging on the edge wondering whether or not you can continue on this journey of change, know that it's likely you are right on the edge of a breakthrough. Don't stop now!

Is there anything right now that is hindering you? Is there anything you need to work on? Is there anything that's keeping you from being responsive? Is your heart responsive toward the things of God? Have you grown hard and no longer respond?

Maybe you've done things your own way so long that you don't know how to live any other way. Maybe you've gone down your own road far enough that you're not sure whether you can turn back. And maybe you're so far beyond being humble and responsive that you've just given up trying.

> The most significant thing you can do to prepare for change is to check your life's alignment.

I want you to know that God's not finished with you. The journey isn't over. There is hope. If I could make the change before I had to, so can you. I promise. I've already told you I'm not superhuman. I'm a human being just like you. If God can work through me, He can work through you, too.

God wants to take away the hardness of your heart. He wants to give you a responsive heart like Josiah had. The Bible says that there was not a king before Josiah who had been as responsive as he was to God (see 2 Kings 23:25). Wow! Could someone say that about you?

I want to be like Josiah. I want you to be like him. I want you to have a responsive heart. I want that to be an accurate description of your life. It can be. I believe it can. I know it can. Do you believe?

The most important step you can take right now is to align your faith with your decisions. Make sure that what you believe to be truth is, in fact, God's truth. And when you know that what you put your faith in is God's truth, then you should make decisions that are consistent with that truth.

This is where we miss it. Our faith is not in recovery programs. They're great! I love recovery programs. But there's no magic there. Our faith is not in psychology or counseling. I love the study of psychology, and I so appreciate professional counselors. But there's no power there. Our faith is not in our spouse or our children. I love family, and I support marriage. But there's not enough your spouse or children can do for you to help you make the change before you have to. The power of faith comes through our decisions to believe in God and to act on what we know to be true from His Word.

When we align this faith with our decisions, then our humility, our commitment to action, and our responsiveness combine to push us toward different and better decisions. Change begins with making different decisions and choosing to respond to situations and circumstances differently than we had before.

My prayer for you right now is that you will have a responsive heart. If your heart has been hard, I pray God will start to soften it so you will change before you have to, not because you have to. I know it can happen for you.

I'm so glad you've decided to read this book because I know that God has a plan for you that is more than who and what you are right now. I want you to think about Josiah, whom everyone counted out. His dad was not a good king, he was young, and he had all the odds stacked against him. In spite of all that, he didn't give up. He chose to change.

Josiah made the change, beat all the odds, and aligned his faith with his decisions. As a result, God used him in a powerful way. Do you believe that God can do the same thing in you? I do. And the reason I do is because He did that work in me, too.

Josiah had something within him that allowed him to lead people and change before he had to. When confronted with God's truth, he was humble. Josiah took action and had a responsive heart. That's what you need to develop in your life if you are going to change before you have to.

We don't know better than God; God knows better than us. It's time we established the role of godly faith in our lives—and in our decisions. It's time to listen to the people in our lives who know us better than we know ourselves and have been begging us to change. There is a better way. God's way is better, and I pray that you will have a responsive heart.

If your heart is a rock, I hope the rest of this book will soften it. If you've stopped listening, stopped striving, or stopped reaching for the change you need to make because you think it's impossible, I hope something in the rest of this book will pull you forward and give you the strength to take those difficult first steps.

When we align our faith with our decisions, something unbelievable happens; change becomes possible. Why? Because we aren't acting with our own strength. God begins to work within us. Hear the whisper of the Holy Spirit; repent, respond, and move forward. Just with a whisper God can help you develop a responsive heart that aligns your faith with your decision to act with urgency, commitment, and conviction.

CHAPTER 10 IN REVIEW

Key Ideas

- When our values—or faith—is out of line with our decisions, we can do significant damage to our lives before we realize it.

- If you're hanging on the edge wondering whether or not you can continue on this journey of change, know that it's likely you are right on the edge of breakthrough.

- When we align our faith with our decisions, then our humility, our commitment to action, and our responsiveness combine to push us toward different and better decisions.

- We don't know better than God; God knows better than us.

- The most important step you can take right now is to align your faith with your decisions.

Discussion Questions

1. What do you think it means to align your faith with your decisions?

2. On a scale of one to ten (one being the lowest and ten being the highest), how would you rate your life's alignment with your faith?

3. When did you stop believing that change was possible in your life? Do you still believe that? Why? Why not?

4. Why do we think we know more than God? How is this reflected in the decisions that we make?

5. Name a couple of people you know who beat all the odds and made significant changes in their lives. How did they do it? What were their experiences like? If you don't know the whole story, invite them to share that with you.

SECTION THREE

OVERCOME THE OBSTACLES TO CHANGE

Chapter 11

RESIST THE COMFORT OF OLD HABITS

Obstacles. Just the mention of the word brings to mind specific situations and people. As we move forward in life, obstacles become the markers for significant decisions. We know that's true because we've seen it played out throughout history. The desire to change will bring us face to face with obstacles. Unless we face and conquer the obstacles in our lives, there will be no change. We will retreat into the most recent place of comfort and security.

I want to talk to you about overcoming the obstacles to change. Change and obstacles go together like peanut butter and jelly. We don't just bump into obstacles; they seem to throw themselves at us. It happens every time.

I decided I needed to change physically. I looked at my life and said, "My marriage is going great, my parenting is going great, my spiritual life's going great, I'm a really great boss!" Of course, all my staff said, "Amen."

Then I looked in the mirror and saw the change I needed to make. I needed to physically change because my physical body was a mess. My body fat percentage was too high. The doctor said I was a heart attack waiting to happen. Most of my body fat was around my waist. and in my face. Something had to be done. So I went to work on it. Immediately the obstacles started tracking me down.

I am making progress toward achieving my goal, but it's not easy. Change never is. I actually did a video journal to document the change I was making, and it's funny to see how many obstacles came my way!

God wants us to change some things in our lives. I don't know what God wants to change in your life, but I am certain He wants you to change in some way. God wants you to change every day and become more like Him. Only you know the change you need to make. Maybe it's physical, maybe it's your marriage, maybe it's your purity, or maybe it's your mouth that's getting you into trouble.

I can't even begin to imagine what you need to change because there are so many different areas of life that need improving. God doesn't want us to focus all of our energies on changing others because that's out of our control; He wants us to change the things *we* can change. Most often, we can only change ourselves.

When we try to change anything, we're going to face obstacles. I was trying to change my weight by working out and making the right choices. My struggles and obstacles were real.

I struggled with eating the right things. I had to replace unhealthy food choices with healthy options. This was particularly hard when traveling. I knew I couldn't go into a restaurant and order the same things I had always ordered. I knew what not to eat; I didn't know what I should eat. So I did something about it and bought the book *Eat This, Not That* by David Zinczenko. It was a great place to start.

This was the first time in my life I had intentionally set out to live a healthy lifestyle and eat healthy foods. It wasn't as easy as I thought it would be. There were times when I just wanted to give up and go back to doing what I had been doing most of my life. But I knew what that had produced. I was an oversized testimony to the power of bad choices.

I remember when I went out for lunch and ordered salmon for the very first time. Salmon had never been a choice on my menu. Almonds became my favorite snack, and protein drinks were discovered! I started swimming for exercise and thought my lungs were going to explode. I started feeling anxious about Thanksgiving and the bountiful, bad foods that would tempt me. What would I do?

Even though I had set specific goals to get my weight under control and was determined to meet them, I made some poor choices. I ate too much of the wrong things. When that happened, I simply had to get right back on the program and get moving in the right direction again.

> Change and obstacles go together like peanut butter and jelly.

As the weeks passed, it got easier to make the right choices. I started looking forward to exercise. Eating healthy wasn't so hard. I had victorious moments when I passed by the dessert display without salivating on the glass case. And there were moments when I lacked good judgment.

My wife was an incredible source of support and encouragement. It's almost impossible to pursue change alone! It's amazing how much one other person's encouragement can help you make the right choices.

Can you identify with the struggle? You want to change, you try to change, but change doesn't happen. The apostle Paul puts it this way: "I do not understand what I do. For what I want to do I do not do, but what I hate I do" (Rom. 7:15). Can you relate to Paul's struggle?

How do we overcome the obstacles we face? If we are going to change before we have to, we must resolve to overcome the obstacles. Many of us need a wake-up call to get us to change. The situation is dangerous. Sometimes, however, we wait until it's too late. You have the heart attack, your spouse decides to leave, your kid chooses to run away, the creditor starts to call. There must be a motivation to change. You can change in response to a bad situation, or you can change before you have to. The wise person will choose the latter. Proverbs 27:12 says, "The prudent see danger and take refuge, but the simple keep going and suffer for it."

There are some great wake-up calls in the Bible. I believe God has some creativity with His wake-up calls and He knows how to get us to change.

Saul—who later became the apostle Paul—was persecuting the church. Only after God knocked him off his donkey and caused him to go blind for several days did he decide to change (see Acts 9:1–9).

We all remember the story of Jonah and the big fish. Jonah was supposed to go to Nineveh to preach. He did not want to go to Nineveh. He hated the people there, because they were so violent and evil. So he went the opposite direction and got on a boat headed as far away from Nineveh as he could go. God provided him a little wake-up call—a storm. During the storm, the sailors threw Jonah overboard. Jonah was swallowed by a big fish. Three days in the belly of a fish got Jonah's attention. Once freed from his gastric jail cell, Jonah decided that going to Nineveh was a good idea after all. (See Old Testament, book of Jonah.)

Nebuchadnezzar was the king of Babylon. In Daniel chapter 4, the Bible tells us that Nebuchadnezzar said, "I am great. I am amazing. Look at how much I have made and look at how great my kingdom is and look at how awesome I am." Daniel went to him and said, "God is not happy with your pride. God wants you to change, or He will humble you. He will humble you and you will crawl on all fours like a cow and you will eat grass for years." Nebuchadnezzar was thinking, *Okay, alright, I'm not going to really say that God's number one. I'm not going to do that.*

Nebuchadnezzar looked out over his kingdom and said, "Look at what I have made. Look at how good this is. Look at how awesome I am." Those words no sooner left his lips that he fell down on all fours and went out in the pasture and started mooing. That was a bad day! Do you think God got his attention? He should have changed before he had to!

God will use things in your life to wake you up, but it's always better to change before you have to. This makes most people say, "I want to change. I no longer want this habit to control my life. I no longer want to be bound by this. I am going to change." As soon as you say that, the obstacles start coming after you. You start saying the same thing the apostle Paul did in Romans 7:20–21, "Now if I do what I do not want to do, it is no longer I who do it, but it is sin living in me that does it. So I find this law at work: Although I want to do good, evil is right there with me." Did you catch that? "Evil is right there with me." And then he says in verse 25, "Thanks be to God, who delivers me through Jesus Christ our Lord!"

Obstacles most often are the work of an outside force: the enemy of your soul. You have an enemy. When you decide to live for God, you become an enemy of the Devil. I believe in the Devil. I believe that he's real. He's not a little red cartoon guy. He's real and he hates you and he wants to steal, kill, and destroy the very good things that are in your life (see John 10:10). When you say you want to change, you want to follow Jesus, he comes against you.

First John 4:4 says, "The one who is in you is greater than the one who is in the world." And you can overcome the Devil. But you try to change and he comes against you saying, "You can't change, it won't happen, you can't do it." So you are going to have to fight for your change. You are going to have to overcome these obstacles. But there's a problem. We live in a society that isn't very conducive to change for the good. Everywhere we are surrounded with encouragement to make bad choices. Change will require you to fight the obstacles because the danger of staying the way you are is more threatening than the battle you must fight.

Let's take a closer look at a common obstacle—the comfort of old patterns. Whether it's good or bad, you do a lot of things a certain way simply because you've always done them that way. You may know something is wrong, but it's comfortable, so you keep doing it. I had a lot of pleasure and comfort from Little Debbie snack cakes and plenty of other sugar snacks. (By the way, they are no longer in my pantry.) Every night before I went to bed, I'd grab a glass of milk and a Little Debbie snack cake. I knew it was bad for me, but I had grown comfortable with it. It was my pattern.

You've grown comfortable with your patterns. You've grown comfortable with your issues—even your sin. You've grown comfortable with a bad marriage. You've grown comfortable with it because you have your agreement. You do your stuff and she does her stuff. You know that it's not right and you know that it's not good, but you've grown comfortable with your old pattern. Change would take work, so you don't want to change. You'd rather stay comfortable in your old habit, keep doing the same thing, because it's going to be painful and it's going to take hard work to make a change, and you prefer the comfort of your old ways.

> Change is hard, but God's plan is always better.

You need to remind yourself that change is hard, but God's plan is always better. It might be more comfortable to stay where you are and to keep going along with what you're doing, but God's plan is better. It might be harder, but it is better. I was comfortable with my body fat. I was comfortable with high cholesterol. But I was a heart attack waiting to happen. And it wouldn't have been very comfortable the day I was rushed to the hospital. After the heart attack—if I lived through the heart attack—my life would be extremely uncomfortable.

Our comfort today sometimes prevents us from making the change we need to make. Don't be comfortable with a destructive habit. Daniel chapter 4 points out the dangers of Nebuchadnezzar's comfort. It says, "I, Nebuchadnezzar, was at home in my palace, contented and prosperous. I had a dream that made me afraid" (Dan. 4:4–5). The dream made him afraid. The dream was his call to change before he had to. But he was content and prosperous. He probably thought, *"Who is Daniel? Who is his god, I mean, really? And look at how good I have it! Look at how good! Everybody fears me, everybody bows before me! If I say that God's number one and I'm not, I might lose some of my comfort. I might lose some of my authority. No, I'm not going to say that. I'm comfortable. I'm going to stay right here."* We do the same thing.

If you're going to overcome your obstacles, you're going to have to overcome what you've grown comfortable with. Otherwise, you will stay stuck in that destructive rut.

CHAPTER 11 IN REVIEW

Key Ideas

- Moving forward in life will always involve overcoming obstacles.

- Facing obstacles is not a sign of spiritual weakness; being defeated by obstacles is.

- God often gives us wake-up calls to encourage us to change before we have to.

- Our old patterns, or ways of life, can interfere with our desire to change.

- When we view our lives from God's perspective, we should become uncomfortable with certain aspects. These are the areas we need to change first.

Discussion Questions

1. Describe a time when you faced an obstacle. How did you deal with it?

2. What are some of the powerful obstacles in your life?

3. Has God ever given you a wake-up call? If so, what was the situation? If not, in what area of life might God be ready to give you a wake-up call?

4. What is the role of your relationship with God and with others in pursuing long-term change in your life?

5. What do you want to be said about you in regard to the changes you need to make in your life? Are you living in a way to earn those comments?

Chapter 12

RECOGNIZE YOUR
LACK OF INFORMATION

We aren't as smart as we think we are. The availability of information in our modern world makes us believe we are experts in every area of life. If we're not feeling well, we can jump on the Internet and self-diagnose the problem, cook up a homemade cure, and be back at work in a few hours. We have become armchair attorneys, physicians, entrepreneurs, inventors, advisors, theologians, counselors, and educators. This leads us to think we have all of the information we need to deal with anything we encounter. This is the way we live, but is it the best way?

Change will require you to identify and overcome ignorance and bad thinking. When I started trying to change my eating habits, I discovered something significant that I hadn't realized up to that point. I didn't know the right foods to eat. I knew about fruits and vegetables. But beyond that, I didn't know anything. My old ways of thinking were simple. I'd go into a store and get whatever I wanted. I never paid attention to the nutritional information. I was ignorant of the things I should eat and how I could make better food choices. The information I needed was right before my eyes all the time. I just never took the time to educate myself. I was ignorant, therefore, I had to get some new knowledge. I had to admit something about myself. I was making bad choices and didn't know how to make better ones.

When you begin looking for new information about the struggle you are facing and how to make better decision, go to the Bible before you read self-help books. God's Word is full of new information that is relevant to your life. In addition, there probably are Bible studies and small groups that will put you in community with other believers so you can get the knowledge you need.

You've also got to fight against the old ways of thinking. Let me illustrate this with my issue. I went to the health club and got a trainer to help me. He actually helped me out two times and has since kept working with me. When I met with him the first time he said, "What are you doing?" I said, "I'm doing a little cardio." He responded, "Good." Then he asked, "What else are you doing?" I said, "I'm doing some bench pressing." Every guy in the gym has to do some bench pressing, right? He asked, "Anything else?" I confessed, "No." And he probed, "So, why are you doing that?" I had to admit that I didn't know why I was doing what I was doing. I did it because that's what you're supposed to do. He mused, "I know why you're doing that. You want to walk around and go, 'Look at the guns, look at the guns. I can bench this much!'" I was busted. That's not what I wanted. Okay, yes it was.

> Change will require you to identify and overcome ignorance and bad thinking.

I had given in to old thinking! My trainer challenged me, "If you want to change, you have to use some new thinking!" I knew that. That truth is foundational to spiritual development. You have to have new thinking, because if you don't put new stuff in, you keep going back to your old patterns.

Apparently I knew that in my head, but I didn't act like I knew any better! Do you know how many times I've tried to workout in my life, and I did the same things: bench press, curls, crunches, a little cardio? I never made any progress. The trainer pressed on, "You've got to do the old, small things that will stabilize your body. You've got to do the foundational things. Your body wants to change, but you need to do it in the right way, and you need some new thinking."

I was asking myself, *Why didn't I get the trainer's help the first week? How many more pounds would I have lost? Or how much better would I feel? And how much further along would I be?*

And some of you need to break out of your old thinking. It's wrong. You default back to the old thinking and you have to break out of that. Look at where you are in life. Your present situation is the result of past decisions and ways of thinking.

You can predict your future with amazing accuracy if you choose to keep thinking the way you've been thinking. Your future will be nothing more than a continuation of your past.

Stop for a moment and look back over the past year. Think about your spiritual development, physical condition, financial picture, employment status, relational health, etc. Where were you in each area twelve months ago? How does your present reality compare to where you were? Have things improved, gotten worse, stayed the same?

Will you be satisfied in each area if nothing changes over the next twelve months? That's the best you can hope for unless you are willing to change your thinking. You will not lose weight if you keep eating like you're eating and refuse to exercise. You will not be better off financially if you maintain the same income level and keep spending like you're spending. Your marriage won't get better by itself. Your kids will not suddenly decide to start communicating with you. Your employer will not apologize for working you like a pack mule.

You are a victim of your own thinking. You aren't a victim of anything else. That's a lie the world wants you to believe. The world wants you to think you can have different results without making any changes. When that happens, you become dependent on external sources for everything. The problem with your situation isn't *out there;* the problem is the common element found in every struggle you face—you!

These are hard truths to swallow because we like to blame others for our problems. That's the way the world thinks. However, that's not the way God wants us to think.

God's Word isn't a source for advice on how to live your life; it is *the* source. Many people, however, consult the Bible only to the point where it challenges their thinking. Then they close it and turn to a source that will tell them what they want to hear. They don't want to change; they want to feel okay about doing things their way.

The Bible addresses every situation in life specifically or in principle. The advice the Bible offers is as valid and relevant in our time as it was two thousand years ago. Most of us have instant access to the entirety of God's Word in multiple versions. Yet, we don't really know what it has to say about our lives and the way we live.

You need information. But it must be reliable, dependable, God-honoring information. That isn't found on the Internet. Hollywood won't provide it. The media isn't interested in giving this kind of information to you. This information is found in one place and one place alone—the Bible.

CHAPTER 12 IN REVIEW

Key Ideas

- Faulty thinking can be corrected only when we obtain accurate information.

- If you've been seeking solutions to your struggles anywhere other than God's Word, you've been taking in false information.

- When God's Word is our primary, authoritative source for information regarding how to live, we will make better decisions and be better prepared to respond when God calls us.

- God's Word addresses every issue we face either specifically or in principle.

- The best thing you can do to obtain better information is to spend quality time studying and digesting God's Word.

Discussion Questions

1. What are some areas of life that you'd like to address with biblical truth?

2. Think about the amount of time you spend on social media, the Internet, watching television, reading books and magazines, listening to music, and reading the Bible. Based on the hours invested in each one, which has the greatest influence on your thought processes?

3. When faced with a decision, how quickly do you turn to God's Word for advice?

4. Who are some people from whom you could gain biblical insight into your life situation?

5. Describe a problem-solving process you would like to use whenever you are faced with a challenge or decision.

Chapter 13

RECONSIDER FRIENDSHIPS

Relationships are messy. If we moved to the woods and lived as recluses, the problem wouldn't go away. We'd probably grow tired of ourselves and begin disliking us. The Bible is clear about the importance of others in our lives.

Again I saw something meaningless under the sun:

There was a man all alone;
he had neither son nor brother.
There was no end to his toil,
yet his eyes were not content with his wealth.
"For whom am I toiling," he asked,
"and why am I depriving myself of enjoyment?"
This too is meaningless—
a miserable business!

Two are better than one,
because they have a good return for their labor:
If either of them falls down,
one can help the other up.
But pity anyone who falls
and has no one to help them up.
Also, if two lie down together, they will keep warm.
But how can one keep warm alone?
Though one may be overpowered,
two can defend themselves.
A cord of three strands is not quickly broken (Eccl. 4:7–12).

Our relational circle has an effect on the direction and speed of our lives. Our friends can encourage our relationships with God or they can interfere. They can encourage us to change or they can talk us into doing what we've always done.

When it comes to friends, you are either influencing them or they are influencing you. Therefore, you need to be careful about the friends you choose. When you are trying to change, there will be friends who are on your side. There also will be people who want to discourage you. Why? They don't want to see that change is possible. Because when people they know change, they feel pressured to change, too. Nowhere was that more evident than in the pagan culture of the biblical town of Corinth.

The culture in Corinth was similar to the world in which we live. Paul wrote to believers there to encourage them to keep themselves unpolluted by the moral decay that was so prevalent. Though this passage is often used in the context of marriage, it is really intended for every relationship. Paul wrote, "Do not be yoked together with unbelievers. For what do righteousness and wickedness have in common? Or what fellowship can light have with darkness?" (2 Cor. 6:14).

Paul's words aren't contradictory to Jesus' call for us to share the gospel with the world. It's one thing to engage people in conversation; it's another thing to be "yoked together." Paul's word picture describes oxen connected with a wooden yoke. The yoke kept the oxen moving together and served to harness their energy. The oxen went everywhere together. By job assignment, they were best friends.

When we are yoked together with unbelievers, we move where they move, which limits our strength. We can't pull away and get back to doing what we know we are supposed to do. Though we don't realize it, we make subtle changes. We talk about what they talk about. We go where they want to go. We do what they want to do. Meanwhile, our effectiveness for God is compromised. Even if we don't violate biblical principles, we're still off the path we should be on.

Proverbs 13:20 says, "Walk with the wise and become wise, for a companion of fools suffers harm." Look closely at that verse. Wisdom is always associated with God. Therefore, when we are friends with godly people, we will be strengthened in our walk with God. But look at what happens when we associate with fools—people who are the opposite of godly. We don't become fools. We suffer harm. It's guilt by association. When their lives derail, we can get caught up in the catastrophe. The Bible is clear. When we become friends with ungodly people, we reflect poorly on our relationship with God and we put ourselves in a position to suffer harm.

Friends also can pull us down. First Corinthians 15:33 says, "Don't be misled—bad company corrupts good character." That's true! Some of you need to tell your story to your friends. You need to say, "Listen, I'm changing! I no longer want to go there anymore." Real friends will support you in your decision to change. If your friends listen to your story and accept

> When it comes to friends, you are either influencing them or they are influencing you.

the changes you desire—stay in those relationships. But if your friends won't accept it and say things like, "No, you're going to come down, you're going to stay running with us," you must be willing to lose those friends. You're going to have to be strong enough to say, "I am going to overcome this obstacle. I love our friendship, but you are bringing me down. And until you are willing to endorse the changes that I am making, I have got to separate." That is just the reality of it—some of you will have to lose some friends.

Some of you need to become better friends with people who are trying to make changes. You need to support them in their efforts to improve their health, marriages, finances, parenting skills, etc. Help them by praying with them and praying for them. Send them encouraging cards and messages. I can't tell you how much it meant when people said, "Are you losing weight? You look good!" Don't take shopaholics to the mall. Don't invite spouses who are working on their marriages to a girls' or guys' night out. Don't take people who are trying to lose weight to the all-you-can-eat buffet. Be a friend, not an obstacle.

This principle is relevant to almost every area of life. You and I have an incredible amount of influence. People watch us and do what we do. They see our choices and choose the same. They model their behavior after ours. Our most significant circle of influence is with our children and immediate family. If you don't want your kids to do it, don't do it. If you don't want your kids addicted to it, don't drink it or smoke it. If you don't want your kids wasting time on the Internet, put the computer away and engage them in conversation.

We have an awesome responsibility to other people. It's not about us. Paul understood that. He was asked about eating meat sacrificed to idols. The meat was the prime cut. It was barbecued as an offering to a meaningless statue or idol. Some believers wanted to know if eating that meat was okay. Why should they throw away good meat? In 1 Corinthians 8:13, Paul wrote, "Therefore, if what I eat causes my brother to fall into sin, I will never eat meat again, so that I will not cause him to fall."

This sheds a new light on things we choose to do that we believe have no effect on anyone but us. We should refrain from anything that might cause someone to misunderstand God and our relationship with Him. This calls into question a lot of activities that the Bible doesn't include on the "do not do these things" list. It doesn't matter whether an activity is on that list. If it might cause people to misunderstand God and His plan for their lives, don't do it. It's that simple.

Is this too restricting? Not really. Adam and Eve had total freedom in the Garden of Eden, except for that one tree (see Gen. 2:15–17). Rather than enjoy the incredible freedoms they had, they focused on the one thing they were instructed to avoid. When we focus on what we should avoid, we become more prone to do it. If we will focus on the incredible freedom we have because of our relationship with God, the things we shouldn't do won't bother us.

Guard rails are placed along the road to protect us from danger. The rails actually are in the safe zone so that hitting the rails will prevent us from encountering the danger. God has placed His guard rails in our lives to keep us from danger. When we bump into God's principles, we should bounce back to the center of the road and keep moving. We don't have to go off the side of the road and crash. God's principles serve to protect us and keep us living in the freedom that He wants us to have. There is incredible freedom in knowing God. Many people, however, choose to think about the prohibitions. Doing so prevents them from living in the freedom.

> God's principles serve to protect us and keep us living in the freedom that He wants us to have.

If I tell you not to think about vanilla ice cream, you'll think about vanilla ice cream. However, if I tell you to think about being healthy and fit, vanilla ice cream doesn't enter the picture. When it comes to our relationships, we must focus on the positive aspects, not the negatives, and be willing to walk away from any relationship that interferes with our walk with God.

Look at 1 Corinthians 15:33 again: "bad character corrupts good morals." In other words, you become like the people you hang around with. Be careful. Don't think you can make someone your best friend and not be affected. There are too many horror stories of people who developed a personal or physical relationship before they connected spiritually.

Look around most churches today and you'll see a lot of women who attend without their husbands. Why? Are the husbands losers? Possibly! No, seriously, many women fell in love and thought they could change their "dream guy." Now, ten years and three kids later, he's still not interested in spiritual matters. If they had connected spiritually to begin with, things might be different.

Now, however, they are living with the consequences of an unwise chain of events. I'm not saying they shouldn't have married. I'm just saying that they should have thought about this aspect of life before they got married. We should pray for people in that situation because God is in the restoration business.

We also should look at our own lives and see the future through the lens of impending decisions. Surround yourself with the friends you need to help you so you can change before you have to.

CHAPTER 13 IN REVIEW

Key Ideas

◆ The people you choose to spend time with will influence your ability to change.

◆ The Bible tells us to avoid being "yoked" with unbelievers. This is a challenge to view your social circles and make some tough calls.

◆ When our main pursuit in life is fellowship with God, change will be natural. When our pursuit is fellowship with people, change will be difficult.

◆ We should refrain from anything that might cause someone to misunderstand God and our relationship with Him.

◆ We have a responsibility to support and encourage people who are pursuing positive change in their lives.

Discussion Questions

1. On a scale of one to ten, how would you rate the quality of your three most important relationships?

2. Thinking back on the three relationship rated above, what is your role in each one? Are you primarily the influencer or the influenced? Explain your response.

3. What is the spiritual atmosphere of the three relationships? Cold, lukewarm, hot? How can you make or keep these relationships focused on knowing and honoring God?

4. Who in your circle of influence is trying to make a significant life-change? How can you support and encourage this person?

5. Who is supporting you in your pursuit of significant life-change? How important to your success is that support?

Chapter 14

IGNORE THE URGE TO GIVE UP

God does not want us to slip up. It is not His plan for us to slip. But if we live in the real world, we all know that we all fall from time to time. I don't want to slip, I don't want to mess up . . . but I do. We can't just excuse ourselves because we agree that everyone will make mistakes. That shouldn't keep us from pursuing perfection, even though we know it's not possible. There's a battle going on. It's been going on since the Garden of Eden. It's a battle that you deal with every day of your life.

It's a battle between the flesh and the spirit, fighting against each other. The flesh is our natural, sinful nature. The spirit is the new nature we receive when we accept Jesus' offer of forgiveness and make Him our Lord. If you feed the flesh, you're going to yield to the flesh. If you feed the Spirit, you're going to yield to the Spirit. Simple equation, right? (See Prov. 15:14 and Gal. 5:17.)

How do we feed the flesh? Look at it this way: There are two categories of things in the world, and everything fits into one of these categories. First, there are things that move us away from God or redirect our eyes from

Him. Of course, the other category is the things that move us toward God and put our eyes on Him. When you look at your day, the category that occupies the most time wins that day. We feed the flesh when we engage in conversations we shouldn't engage in, when we look at things online we shouldn't look at, when we eat foods we shouldn't eat, listen to music that imbeds impure thoughts in our minds, think more about ourselves than others, spend more time reading Facebook than God's Word. (Get the picture?) Many of us have been feeding the flesh way too much. That's when we slip up. So when we slip, what happens?

If you take your eyes off of God while pursing change, you might slip up and fall off the wagon. It should bother you. You'll feel down. At that point, you cannot listen to the voice of the enemy. He will come after you saying something like this: "Change? Change nothing! You are a failure! Look at you—you've failed again! Now stay down and don't get up. Don't even think you're a Christian. You call yourself a Christian? A Christian would never do that."

That voice will lie to you and say, "Don't go to church. They don't want people like you at church. Don't go to church. You're a failure! Quit your small group! Don't even tell them what's going on!"

That's what the voice tells you. It lies to you! When you're down, you start thinking, *"I can never . . . I'm a failure . . . Jesus would never forgive . . . Jesus is so mad . . . He's kicking me out. I'm done for. I'm never, ever finding forgiveness."*

Many people believe those lies and let them start rolling around in their heads. They feel guilty. Sometimes guilt leads to the conviction that they're wrong and they repent—that's where they're supposed to go.

But some people wallow in guilt. They stay down. They say, "I'm not getting up. It's over. I'm no good. I'm terrible. I am staying down." That's a defeated position, and God never intended for you to stay there.

Let me tell you something I've learned to do. I've learned to be a "quick confessor." I think this can really help a lot of people. What do I mean by that? When I fall in any area—and I don't live a perfect life—I truly repent of it. I say, "God, I am sorry. I am sorry for what I have done wrong. And

I am changing and I am moving forward with you. And I am not going to stay down in guilt. I'm going to ask for your forgiveness. And I know that Your Word is true—that You will forgive me of my unrighteousness, You will cleanse me from it, and I'm going to move forward in Your victory."

Then I get right back up. I don't wallow in that guilt. And I start moving forward to where I want to go. I tell myself, "I'm not going to be defined by my guilt. I'm not going to be defined by what I did. That was a slip, and I'm not a failure . . ."

A lot of us can't do that. We are not quick confessors. We beat ourselves up, and we beat ourselves up, and we beat ourselves up, over and over. We hear our mom's voice, our dad's voice, a teacher's voice, a boss's voice, the voice of the enemy, and we just beat ourselves up and we walk around defeated. We don't realize that if we confess our sins and repent God has forgiven us, and He says, "Now, get up and move on! Move forward and be who I want you to be." This is what Jesus said to the woman He saved from being stoned to death after she was caught in adultery (John 8:10–11):

> God did amazing things with flawed people.

> Jesus straightened up and asked her, "Woman, where are they? Has
>   no one condemned you?"
> "No one, sir," she said.
> "Then neither do I condemn you," Jesus declared. "Go now and
>   leave your life of sin."

The enemy will use every memory in your mind to convince you that you are a loser. On the authority of God's Word, let me tell you, you are not a loser! This is what we read in 1 John 1:9: "If we confess our sins, he is faithful and just and will forgive us our sins and purify us from all unrighteousness."

Except for Jesus, there is no one in the Bible who never failed. It started with Adam and Eve and continued through the first century AD. God did amazing things with flawed people. He led the people out of Israel with a reluctant leader who had committed murder. He put an end to the Philistine antagonism using a young boy and a slingshot. A prostitute gave shelter to God's spies and ended up in Jesus' genealogy. A demon-possessed man got set free and became a missionary! A Jesus-hater became the most powerful missionary in history. He wants to keep doing great things through us (see Hebrews 11).

The enemy doesn't want that to happen. He wants us to be defeated and useless. He knows that guilt will take us out of the game and put us on the sidelines. When we sit on the bench, Satan is delighted.

Go back and think about the individual stories of Abram, Moses, David, Samson, Gideon, Peter, and others. (If you don't know them, I encourage you to read them and be encouraged!) They failed God, but they refused to let their failures define them. They accepted forgiveness but never escaped the consequences of their sin and continued doing what God called them to do. You can't let your failure stop you either. When you get back up and become a quick confessor, you realize that this whole walk with God is from grace and He will give you the grace to make the change!

There are no perfect people; there are only broken people who serve a perfect God. If we believe perfection is required by God, we all are disqualified. God wants us to honor Him with our lives and pursue His best for us. He has a plan that is the best plan for our lives. As we pursue a strong relationship with Him, we will be better able to see His plan. We can't see His plan, however, if we keep our distance from Him. Jeremiah 29:11 reads, "'For I know the plans I have for you,' declares the LORD, 'plans to prosper you and not to harm you, plans to give you hope and a future.'"

> There are no perfect people; there are only broken people who serve a perfect God.

The pursuit of God is a lifelong adventure. It culminates in our arrival in heaven when we die. Until then, we have an awesome responsibility to serve God and change according to His promptings and desires for us. God doesn't call us to change just to give us something to do. He calls us to change because He wants you and me to make Him famous through our lives.

There is something in each of us that needs to change. There is some aspect of our lives that needs to be conformed to God's image. It might be a big deal; it might be something small. Unless we are perfect, there is something. Take the time to identify what God wants to change in your life. Don't give up if you fall off the wagon. God's purpose is more important than your pride. Get up. Get moving. And change before you have to!

CHAPTER 14 IN REVIEW

Key Ideas

- ◆ God doesn't want you to slip up.

- ◆ There is a battle raging between the sinful nature and the Holy Spirit. Sometimes, the sinful nature wins and you do something you know you shouldn't do.

- ◆ When you fail, it's easy to get down on yourself and want to give up. You can't let that happen.

- ◆ The Bible is full of stories of people who slipped up but still were used to accomplish great things for God.

- ◆ You have an awesome responsibility to serve God and change according to His promptings and desires for your life.

Discussion Questions

1. In what areas of life are you most tempted to give in to the sinful nature?

2. Based on the way you spend your time and the people with whom you spend it, which nature are you strengthening more—the sinful nature or the spiritual one? Are you satisfied with your response? Why or why not?

3. Describe a time when you failed but had to pick yourself up and keep going. How did you make that happen?

4. Pick a Bible personality that you connect with and read his or her story. How did that person overcome failure? What can you learn from that story?

5. God is prompting change in your life. In what way does He want you to change? How will that change bring honor and glory to Him?

Chapter 15

VISUALIZE
LIFE AFTER CHANGE

Some people say that visualizing your life after a change is a great motivation for pursuing the change. I agree—if you're going to move ahead, you need to see the future change. There were times when the only thing that kept me moving forward was the mental image of how I would feel when I reached my weight-loss goal. I could see myself fitting into clothes in waist sizes I'd not experienced since college. I could see myself walking from the parking lot to my office without being winded. I could see myself with more energy, less aches and pains, more creativity, more life, and maybe even a better golf swing!

There were days when that vision of my future motivated me to keep moving. I made the right choices. I ate the right foods. I felt good about myself. It all started when I saw myself in the future. The vision made a difference.

Seeing things like that was helpful. But it didn't stop me from falling off the wagon. I remember one situation in particular. I don't tell you this to give you license to jump off your own wagon; I just want you to know that change is hard work.

It was a Thursday in December. I was doing so good. I had stayed on track, watched my diet, and said no to a multitude of temptations. Then it happened. Catherine, the lady who cleans our church, brought in some fresh baked goodies. I knew I didn't need them. So, I decided to take them home for the kids to have for breakfast the following day. (Good excuse, right?)

I fought the temptation throughout the day. That night, I had a meeting that lasted until eleven o'clock. My wife reminded me that I needed to pick up some donuts for my son's choir class the following day. So, I was in the car with fresh baked goodies from Catherine and a box of cake donuts for my son's class. That's a recipe for disaster for someone who is trying to make the right choices about food—especially if that hungry person is famished!

I wasn't prepared for battle. The meeting lasted longer than I thought it would, and I had not eaten all afternoon and not much at dinner that evening. I should have planned better, but I didn't. Since I was really hungry, I started rationalizing partaking of the snacks; not the boxed donuts but the fresh-baked goodies. I indulged. I didn't convince myself eating the goodies was right. I didn't care if it was right. I was hungry, food was available, so I ate. Big deal, right?

The entire time I was enjoying the fresh baked, delicious goodies, I was kicking myself. I knew better. I knew the right choice to make. I could have avoided the entire guilt trip simply by doing what I knew what the right thing to do. I fell off the wagon. At that point, I had lost eight pounds. I had worked out hard. I had been eating right. But that one lapse in judgment cost me more than I imagined.

At a weak moment, I lacked the willpower I needed to fight for what was right. The enemy (my appetite!) wore me down. He knew my vulnerability all too well. He understood my weaknesses. He attacked at the one place he knew my defenses were weak: dessert!

Now don't get me wrong, I wasn't attacked spiritually or morally. I'm certainly vulnerable in those areas too. I was attacked at the one place that defeating me would be easy. Your flesh and other forces will attack you at your weak spot too.

Do not merely listen to the word, and so deceive yourselves. Do what it says. Anyone who listens to the word but does not do what it says is like a man who looks at his face in a mirror and, after looking at himself, goes away and immediately forgets what he looks like. But the man who looks intently into the perfect law that gives freedom, and continues to do this, not forgetting what he has heard, but doing it—he will be blessed in what he does (James 1:22–25).

I knew what to do, and I didn't do it. That's always a recipe for disaster and an opportunity for us to make regrettable decisions. We get comfortable doing things the way we've always done them. We make decisions in predictable ways. We choose to do whatever we like to do.

> You must have a plan of defense in place before you are exposed to temptation.

We don't change because we've grown comfortable doing whatever we like to do. We think it feels good, we think it tastes good, and we think that's who we are and that's what we like. We even grow comfortable with the guilt trip. At first, it bothers us. Eventually, we're not bothered anymore. We brush off our failures as part of the routine. We convince ourselves that failure isn't so bad. We sometimes convince ourselves that God wants us to be happy, so it is fine if we do whatever we want to do.

My problem was food. Your problem might be pornography, gossip, addiction, social media, inappropriate relationships, dishonesty, greed, and so forth. You might have gone through the thinking process I went through. You believe that one more look won't hurt. You masquerade your gossip as "sharing prayer requests." You claim you don't have an addiction because you can quit anytime you want. So, why haven't you?

You think you've got the handle on social media, but you grab your phone to read the latest post without thinking about what you're doing. You have rationalized your affair, excused your greed, and covered one lie with another one. Your life is spinning out of control and everyone knows it, except you. You keep running into these brick walls of temptation and can't seem to escape temptation's snare.

You must have a plan of defense in place before you are exposed to temptation in the area you are trying to change. You want to change. Maybe you are changing. You just need to stay faithful. The change you are making isn't a short-term, temporary change; this is permanent. This is a new way of life.

The Bible tells us, "Flee from sexual immorality. All other sins a man commits are outside his body, but he who sins sexually sins against his own body" (1 Cor. 6:18). Some of you aren't fleeing immorality; you are taking it to dinner and inviting it to live in the guest bedroom. *Flee* comes from the Greek word that means, "run for your life." Okay, I made that up, but that's the image you get from the word. We aren't told to date immorality, we are told to run from it. We aren't told to excuse our bad decisions, we are told to do things God's way. But we still fail, don't we?

Whenever you fall off the wagon, lose your temper, or just blow it, you must remind yourself that there will be better days ahead. God does not want you to stay down when you fall. God wants you to get back up. When the apostle Peter denied Jesus three times, Jesus didn't say, "Peter, you're no good. We're getting somebody else." He let Peter preach to thousands on the day of Pentecost. God does not want you to stay down, God wants you to overcome your obstacles. You know what, He sees in you a victorious man or woman of God. He sees you achieving your potential. He is the voice that speaks into your life and says, "I know you can do it." (That's the voice you need to listen to!)

I believe we all can identify with what the psalmist said in Psalm 94:17–19, "If God hadn't been there for me, I never would have made it. The minute I said, 'I'm slipping, I'm falling,' your love, God, took hold and held me fast. When I was upset and beside myself, you calmed me down and cheered me up" (MSG).

When you say, "Lord, my foot is slipping. Lord, I need some strength," His love will come to you and give you the strength you need to change. God says, "Change before you have to. Become the man or woman of God that I know you can be and change before you have to."

When you visualize yourself after the change, you'll see a better version of you. You'll be more joyful, functional, and relational. You'll be in a position to improve your relationship with God because that thing that has been standing in the way will be minimized.

You need to talk to God and tell Him the change you want to make. Prayer is nothing more than talking to and hearing from God. It's not like talking into the speaker at the drive-thru where we pull up and place our orders. Prayer includes listening to God.

> He sees in you a victorious man or woman of God.

So pray that you will become the man or woman of God that He knows you can be. Don't listen to the voice of the enemy that says you can't change, you're no good, you're unworthy. When you face obstacles, pray for the strength to get though those obstacles, around them, over them, and run away from them.

Ask God to speak to you regarding the area you want to change. It might be physical, emotional, spiritual, or relational. Ask God to give you a vision of what you can be so that you can be courageous and change before you have to.

CHAPTER 15 IN REVIEW

Key Ideas

- One of the most effective motivators for pursuing change is the visualization of yourself after the change.

- If you fall off the wagon, the image of the changed you will help you get back on the wagon and keep moving toward the change.

- God doesn't disqualify people for failing. We disqualify ourselves by refusing to get back up.

- Prayer is two-way communication with God. When we do all the talking, we shut off God's direct line of communication with us.

- When you face obstacles, pray for the strength to get through those obstacles, around them, over them, and away from them.

Discussion Questions

1. What is your vision for your life after the change you are pursuing? What is the most significant aspect of your life that will change?

2. Have you ever set a goal and then quit before reaching it? If so, how did you feel? If not, how have you kept yourself from stopping along the way?

3. What would happen if God disqualified everyone who fails? Who would be left to serve Him?

4. When was the last time you quietly listened to God through prayer? What did He say to you?

5. Write a prayer asking for strength to deal with the obstacles you face. Commit the prayer to memory and be prepared to use it whenever you face an obstacle to change in your life.

SECTION FOUR

PUT ON THE MIND OF CHANGE

Chapter 16

TRUST GOD'S POWER WITHIN YOU

The mind is an interesting thing. Researchers have been trying to figure out how the memory works for many years. They want to know why we can remember our phone number from fifteen years ago but can't remember where we parked our cars twenty minutes ago. They want to know why song lyrics are so easy to remember but sequences of numbers are not.

Speaking of songs, there are certain songs that get stuck in our heads. They often are the most annoying songs with the most ridiculous lyrics. But there's something about them that makes them stick. You try to make them vanish from your memory. You try to force them out by thinking of a different song. It doesn't work.

I know this really bothers my wife. One time we went to a music show in Branson and they performed a really stupid song. Of course, I got in the car and started singing it. She exclaimed, "Great, now it's stuck there forever." So sometimes when I want to tease her, I sing that song again. (For those of you in the early stages of a relationship, don't do that, because you want to stay married for a long time!)

There are plenty of songs that will pop into your head when you read a few words. Give it a try. "Who let the . . ." See, it's there, right? We've got these things that are locked in our brains, and we just can't get rid of them. Even the "ABC" song we sang as children remains stuck in our heads no matter how hard we try to get rid of it! Some of you just started singing it in your heads again.

> God has empowered you to do anything and everything He has called you to do.

As we begin the final section of this book, I want us to think about the power that is within us. Brain researchers tell us that we never really forget anything that is tucked away in our long-term memory. That's why we remember songs from twenty years ago. Setting the words to music and then hearing them over and over solidifies the song in long-term memory. There are other things that are tucked away through rote memorization and multiple exposures.

There are things that we just can't forget because our minds won't let us forget them. There also are things we can't ever seem to remember, but that's a topic for a different book. Our minds are incredible file cabinets. So we never forget information, we just don't know where and how it is stored. When we create a way to "label" information in our minds, we can recall just about anything we've learned.

What's this got to do with making a change? God has empowered you to do anything and everything He has called you to do (see Phil. 4:13). It makes sense, doesn't it? God doesn't call us to perform a task or to make a change just so He can watch us fail, right? Yet, obeying God's instructions can be a big challenge for us.

We think we know what God wants us to do, but we're not sure. So, we go on a quest trying one thing after another hoping that something we do will be what God wants us to do. We wish God would just give us a simple map, an uncomplicated way to know His mind. I've got great news for you: God did just that! And because God did that, we have the promise of a life of abundance, passion, and satisfaction.

Paul's letter to the Philippians contains a very familiar passage, Let's take a closer look at it.

I rejoice greatly in the Lord that at last you have renewed your concern for me. Indeed, you have been concerned, but you had no opportunity to show it. I am not saying this because I am in need, for I have learned to be content whatever the circumstances. I know what it is to be in need, and I know what it is to have plenty. I have learned the secret of being content in any and every situation, whether well fed or hungry, whether living in plenty or in want. I can do everything through him who gives me strength (Phil. 4:10–13).

Read that last line again, except this time make it about the change you want to make. I can change physically though Him who gives me strength. I can overcome my addiction through Him who gives me strength. I can do anything God calls me to do through the strength He provides. It's not impossible for me to change. I can be the person God intended me to be. This battle is winnable.

Paul wasn't overstating his ability; he was expressing his dependence upon God. Look at the verses that precede verse 13. Paul rejoiced in the Lord because the Philippians expressed concern for him. This was a big deal to Paul because he wanted to see spiritual growth in the lives of young believers. This mattered to Paul only because of the intimate relationship he had with God. Investing in the ministry of others is a sign of spiritual maturity and growth.

Paul also learned to be content in any situation. He wasn't looking for bigger or better. This attitude also comes only from an intimate relationship with God. Paul modeled a quality of relationship with God that challenges us to rethink how we relate to Him. We will never be content with what we have until we view what we have from God's perspective.

Because Paul was raised a Jew, he understood the Old Testament promises of God. Because he was an apostle, he understood Jesus' promises. Paul's understanding wasn't just a fleeting awareness; Paul lived the promises. He had seen them in action. He heard God's instructions loud and clear. He was totally aware of the presence of the Holy Spirit in his life. That's why he could say, "I can do everything through him who gives me strength."

We talked about the battle between the sinful nature and the spiritual nature. We already understand that Satan wants us to be defeated and to stay defeated. When we fall, he wants us to stay there because the testimony of your changed life might encourage someone else in his or her relationship with God.

We can't let Satan get in our heads. We need to remind him what the Bible says about him. First John 4:4 says, "The one who is in you is greater than the one who is in the world." Who is in you? The Holy Spirit. Who is in the world? Satan and the forces of evil. The outcome already has been decided. The power within us is greater than the power outside of us.

So, what's the problem? We forget our ammunition. We've heard these Bible promises, but when we try to remember them, we find the words to "Achy Breaky Heart" have taken over our minds. See, there it goes. The words just popped into your head. We have become a culture of religious spectators who don't really know the God we claim to worship or His words.

Many believers are more familiar with popular music lyrics than they are with the Word of God. So, when the enemy comes after them, they are defenseless. They agree with what Satan says about them because he says the same things the songs say. God's truth isn't in the picture. But, it is still truth.

You see, when we let the world tell us what's true, we will scoff at biblical principles and instructions. We will believe the Bible is archaic and out of touch with reality. *What can a book that was written centuries ago possibly tell me about living my life today?* Such thoughts cause us to filter the Bible.

We like the passages about God having a plan for our lives and meeting our needs. We aren't so excited about the passages that call us to live a moral life that is consistent with biblical instruction. We become "buffet Christians." We just roam around picking the elements of belief that will fit into our lives and leave the rest for the "fanatics."

The other approach is to view the world from God's perspective. When that happens, we make judgment calls that might cause our friends to wonder what's going on but will keep us in a right relationship with God. You can't find God's will for your life by living the way you want to live. It doesn't work that way. That only produces frustration and spiritual ineffectiveness. That's not God's plan for your life.

Do you believe that God has the best plan for your life in His hands? Do you believe that He wants you to be victorious over anything that weighs you down? Do you believe He is there to encourage you and equip you to win? So, why don't you live like you believe it? Why don't you let God decide what's right and wrong? Why don't you ask God if what you're about to do will bring honor and glory to Him?

Some people hear that and say, "I'll go to church more." Well, that's a start, but going to church isn't the solution to your problem. Going to church is your opportunity to celebrate what God is doing in and through your life with others who are doing the same. Going to church isn't the same as plugging your electric car into the charging station at the supermarket. This isn't something you do just to get you back home again.

> You have to reorder your priorities and make spending time with Him more important than other things on the list.

If you attend church one hour per week every year of your life from the time you are born until age sixty-five, you will spend a total of four months in church. The average American male during that same span of time will invest nine and a half years watching television. We don't learn to tap into the power of God like that. What happens in church should be an appetizer that makes you want to go home, dig in, and learn more. If you attend church for a spiritual snack, you become spiritually unhealthy.

Church is helpful, but a thriving, vibrant relationship with God is foundational. You can't go through life with a great relationship with your church and a nonexistent relationship with God. It doesn't work that way. God wants to guide your life. He wants to advise you in your decisions. He wants to encourage you in the change you are pursuing. But He won't make you listen to Him. You have to choose to listen. You have to reorder your priorities and make spending time with Him more important than other things on the list.

The power demonstrated in the Bible is God's power through ordinary people. Paul wasn't spiritually superior to others; he was just tuned in to God. Ordinary people did extraordinary things. God has been working in and through ordinary people since the beginning of time.

Here's another key to changing before you have to. You have to memorize Scriptures that will help you fight the battle. I know, I said to memorize Scripture. But you need to do that, because it works! Here's what I mean.

Let's say you are losing the parenting battle (it really can be any battle, but I'm using this one as an example). Memorize some scriptures on parenting and relationships, such as, "Fathers, do not exasperate your children; instead, bring them up in the training and instruction of the Lord" (Eph. 6:4). Or, "A gentle answer turns away wrath, but a harsh word stirs up anger" (Prov. 15:1). When your daughter comes in and asks you a question to which you want to simply say, "I'll think about it," you'll then remember to *not exasperate your child* and instead respond, "Let's talk about it." Or when your teenager is blasting his music, just as you're about to yell at him to turn it down you remember that *a gentle answer turns away wrath,* so you do things differently. This works, but it only works if you memorize God's Word. Your future will look just like your past unless you change, and memorizing the Bible will change your trajectory. Where you are today is the result of decisions you made prior to today. Your future will be the byproduct of the decisions you make today and in the days ahead. If you keep doing what you've been doing, you can be confident you'll stay right where you are. How's that working out for you?

You can make the change. You can do it! And you can make the change because God has given you the power to change before you have to. I believe you can make the change. The key is that we can change our minds and take on a new way of thinking. God has given us the power to do it. Change before you have to.

CHAPTER 16 IN REVIEW

Key Ideas

◆ You never really forget anything that is stored in long-term memory; you just don't know how to find it.

◆ God has empowered you to do anything and everything He has called you to do.

◆ You can change before you have to through God who gives you strength.

◆ Satan and the forces of evil have been defeated. They wield no power over the person who is in an intimate relationship with God.

◆ You can't go through life with a great relationship with your church and a weak relationship with God.

Discussion Questions

1. What are three Bible promises you need to commit to memory?

2. How does it make you feel to know that God has empowered you to do anything and everything He has called you to do?

3. How can you reorder your priorities so you can spend more time with God tapping into His strength?

4. You have the power to overcome Satan and the forces of evil that try to convince you that you are incapable of changing. Which Scripture verses are reminders to you of God's power in and through your life?

5. On a scale of one to ten, with ten being awesome, rate your relationship with your church. Then, using the same scale, rate your relationship with God. Which is stronger? What does this say about your spiritual health?

Chapter 17

TAKE ON
NEW THINKING

You probably do some things a certain way simply because that's the way you've always done them, right? You don't have an explanation. You don't even think about what you're doing. It's just engrained in your mind. It's been there for a long, long time.

Our thinking patterns affect our choices. The way we think controls the way we act. If we think life is all about us, we'll park in the fire lane and take a shopping cart full of groceries through the express lane. We will drive like no one else matters. We'll act rudely toward cashiers and servers. We don't wake up and decide to be self-centered. We're self-centered because our thinking is distorted. If we want to make different choices, we must begin by thinking about our minds and how we think.

Romans 12:1–2 is the key if we're going to change before we have to. This is what it says, "Therefore, I urge you brothers, in view of God's mercy, to offer your bodies as living sacrifices, holy and pleasing to God—this is your spiritual act of worship. Do not conform any longer to the patterns of this world, but be transformed by the *renewing of your mind*. Then you will be able to test and approve what God's will is—His good, pleasing, and perfect will."

God has given us the ability to transform our minds, to change our minds. He said, "Don't be conformed to the old way of thinking, I want you to take on a new way of thinking as you follow Jesus, and you're going to transform your mind."

At a men's event I had the privilege of hearing Mark Laaser speak. He is one of the leading experts in the nation on sexual addictions, and he was addicted to pornography. After deciding that he was going to change, he asked Christ to give him the ability to change his mind and to meditate on God's Word instead of looking at the wrong things anymore. He started looking at God's Word and applying what it said. He said, "God, I'm going to start renewing my mind. I'm going to start putting Your Word into my mind and I'm going to start to change my mind. I want You to change my mind. I want Your Word to be alive in my life and to change my mind in the way I am thinking."

> Our thinking patterns affect our choices. The way we think controls the way we act.

He went to be a part of a test at Vanderbilt University. And while he was there, they hooked him up to all these sensors on his brain. They showed that his brain was thinking a certain way. That he had a pattern in his brain, and his brain was firing off according to a certain pattern. While they had brain sensors on his brain, they showed him the cover of a pornographic magazine. The researchers noted that his brain actually activated a new area. The new area in his brain really was the old path; the old ways of thinking. Once they removed the picture, his brain went back to the new way of thinking with the new part firing.

The researchers remarked, "You know what's amazing? You have retrained your brain. You have retrained your mind. It is now thinking differently because God's Word is active in you. God's Word is true. And you are being transformed."

Isn't it interesting that Vanderbilt University confirmed what Romans 12:1–2 said way before there were brain sensors. So this is true! This is something we can do. We have the power to change before we have to. We can do what God's Word tells us to do. The amazing thing is God is partnering with us. Now grab hold of that—the God of this universe, the God who created everything—He is partnering with you to change your mind. And He's telling you to do something you can actually do. It is not an impossible task. He's telling you that you can do this and He will work with you and help you to change your mind.

Everything you do begins as a thought. Everything follows our head. Everything follows our minds and our thinking. My trainer said, "You know what, turn your head. Everything follows your head. Turn your head and your body will turn there. Turn your head and it will go there."

God is saying, "I want to renew your mind. And as you renew your mind, those other destructive things, they're going to change. Your body is going to change and you're going to renew and you're going to cleanse your mind and things are going to change."

We've got to change our ways of thinking because a lot of us have negative thinking, we have wrong thinking, we have worldly thinking. "Don't be conformed anymore to the pattern of this world." This world has wrong thinking. This world has deadly, destructive thinking. Many of us were raised in it and it has infiltrated our lives. We've got to get rid of those bad thinking processes and start developing new, godly thinking patterns.

I learned this lesson when I was golfing. I would often remind myself that hitting balls into a water hazard wasn't a great plan. I'd think to myself, "Don't hit the ball into the water hazard! Do not! Just get a bad ball, get a bad ball. Because if you hit it into the water hazard, you don't want to lose a good ball. So put a bad ball up there and don't hit that bad ball into the water."

I bet you know what I did. *Boom*—right into the water! So, the next time I was in that situation, I had a little conversation with myself, "Okay, hit a new ball this time. Maybe the new ball will change it. Don't hit the new ball into the water." You guessed it—*boom*—right into the water!

I finally decided to take a ten on that hole. I was done with it. I was ready to move on because I had faulty thinking. We know our thinking is flawed. We know God wants to change our ways of thinking.

What we think is so powerful. Isn't it interesting how much our minds control our actions. The New York Giants were playing the Philadelphia Eagles a couple years ago in a critical game. The Giants were in position to attempt a game winning field goal. And just prior to the kick, the Eagles called a timeout so that the Giants kicker could think about the kick. They hoped his thinking would affect his execution of the kick. They call it "icing the kicker." To help the kicker remember his bad kicks, they put on the Jumbotron every kick that he had missed. The video was complete with commentary, "Oh, he missed it left again," "Oh, he missed it right!" Everyone in the stadium was thinking, *Oh, he misses the kick!* The kicker was prepping for the kick and the whole time they're showing his misses. He just blocked it out by telling himself, "I'm gonna make it, I'm gonna make it, I'm gonna make it."

The ball was snapped and the kick was good. Everyone in the stadium, however, knew how powerful the mind is. That's why God is saying, "I want you to renew your mind. I want you to have new thinking."

CHAPTER 17 IN REVIEW

Key Ideas

- God has given you the ability to transform your mind, to change your mind.

- The key to changing your mind is allowing God to transform your mind.

- Everything you do passes through your brain. If you want to live more like God intends you to live, you must begin by changing your mind and thinking processes.

- It's hard to change your thinking processes because so many things you do are done automatically.

- Without changing your thinking processes, there will be no significant life change.

Discussion Questions

1. What are some thoughts God has changed in your mind?

2. How did God transform your thinking? On a scale of one to five, with five being extremely hard, how difficult was it for God to change your thinking?

3. What are some thinking processes you need to change? What is your plan for allowing God to change them?

4. List three Scripture passages that challenge your thinking processes. When your thinking processes and God's Word disagree, which is right and why?

5. How will your thinking processes change in the process of pursuing the life-change you are pursuing?

Chapter 18

MAKE DIFFERENT DECISIONS

Some of us say, "I can't change. There's no way, I just can't change." You use the excuse, "This is the way I am. I'm too old, I can't change." Let me tell you right now, yes you can change. It's not only possible, it's been proven. And countless people have shown throughout history that we have the ability to change all the way until we die.

We have the ability to change, but people stop changing. Many of us haven't learned anything new in twenty years. We've been doing the same things for longer than we can remember. We buy our groceries at the same place. We get our haircut at the same place. We do everything at the same place. We haven't learned anything new. We haven't memorized a new Scripture. Nothing! Twenty years and we keep doing the same old things and getting the same results. As a result, our brains just start slowing down. Like unused muscles, the brain begins to lose its capacity. It doesn't have to be that way. It is possible to say, "You know what? I'm going to change the way that I am thinking."

I want to share with you a tool created by Dallas Willard. He is a philosophy professor at the University of Southern California, and he is a Christian. He came up with a tool to help us renew our minds. He did it because the Scriptures say we need to renew our minds. That's why the Bible says, "Let this mind be in you that is in Christ Jesus," "Let us have the mind of Christ," and "Let us think on these things." Dallas Willard agrees that our minds must change if we are going to become the people God intended us to become.

Willard created a really interesting, simple tool we can use to renew our minds. It isn't hard to grasp and, by the way, it is useful in other areas of life as well. Here it is: VIM. Have the *vision,* the *intention,* and the *means* to change. Vision. Intention. Means. You have to have all three of these in place to change successfully. (Others have called it Aware, Willing, Able— but it doesn't matter. Just use a tool that can help you remember.)

Here's the deal: You have to have a vision of what you're going to change into. Jesus said that we should want to be like Him. (See Matt 5:48; 16:24; Luke 6:40; John 13:12–17; 1 Cor. 11:1; Eph. 5:1–2; and 1 John 2:4–6.) And so that's our vision. We want to change to be like God, to be more like Christ. That should be our vision and our goal. We should say every day, "God, I want to be more like you, and I have this vision of being a follower of Yours and being more like you. That's what I want to do." That vision should motivate us. It should be something that pumps us up. In response to that vision, we say, "You know what? I want a better life. I want to do what God's Word says. I trust that His Word is true. I've accepted Him as my Lord and Savior. And now I want to be more like Jesus. I have a vision of what I can be as a follower of Jesus Christ."

I think a lot of us don't realize that God wants to give us His kingdom power right now. He wants to give us the power to change. He wants to give us the victorious life. He wants to give us the good promises in His Word. He wants us to be more like Him. He wants us to be able to endure suffering. He wants us to be able to move on and grow.

However, many of us think, *"Everything that God has for us is in heaven. It's all waiting for us there."* And from here until heaven, we struggle through and we don't ever change. Meanwhile, God is saying, "I want to give you that kingdom power right now. I want you to change right now. You can have it. You need to start applying this. I have a vision of what's out there—the better future for you" (see Jer. 29:11).

Interestingly, people who survive heart attacks should have a vision of living longer. They should want to change. But they've found that most people who survive a heart attack understand they need to change or they might die. But they don't change! They think, "Well, my life is pretty miserable already. What do I want to change for? I've got nothing. I don't have a picture of a better future. I mean, I'm depressed right now anyway! That's why I'm not exercising and eating and all this. Life's no good; so change? Why would I want to?"

You know what the doctors have learned? They've learned that fear of something doesn't motivate people to change. The joy of a better future, the joy of the thing before us, is what motivates us to change. My doctor said he's learned this now, and this is how he tells people who have had a heart attack why they should change. He used to tell them if they did not change they were going to die. That didn't help. They wouldn't change.

So now when men have a heart attack my doctor says, "If you don't change, your sex life is going to be taken away from you!" And they go, "Hey, I better change! That's worth changing for!" It's a joy of a better future. (Don't get mad at me. My doctor said this, not me!)

> The joy of a better future, the joy of the thing before us, is what motivates us to change.

But isn't that interesting: the joy of a better future will motivate people to change while fear will not. Note how God's Word describes strength: "The joy of the LORD is our strength" (Neh. 8:10). It doesn't say, "The *fear* of the LORD is our strength." It says, "The *joy* of the LORD is our strength." The joy of making God happy. The joy of living an abundant life. The joy of being what He wants us to be. That's our strength!

Are you catching this? It's a vision of a better future. It's us saying, "God, I want to do what You want me to do, and I want to have the joyful life—the God-filled life—the life that doesn't worry about my outward circumstances." (And let's be honest, some of you are thinking joy means having a big paycheck and a big car and a big house. That's not it.)

Joy is independent of all those outward things. You're saying, "God, I have the joy in my life because I know who I am in You, I know where I'm going, I know that you have a plan for me and a purpose on earth. And I have a vision of making a difference and being more like You as I go through this life. And ultimately, someday, I'm going to be with You in heaven. But, right now, I just want to keep changing and being more like You. I want to make You smile!" The joy of the Lord is our strength!

It's time to change before you have to!

CHAPTER 18 IN REVIEW

Key Ideas

- Until the day we die, we have the ability to change our thinking.

- Our thinking affects our behaviors, therefore, any undesirable behavior can be changed no matter how long it's been going on and no matter how old you are.

- VIM—vision, intention, means—is a helpful tool to navigate change in any area of life.

- God wants to give us His kingdom power right now. We don't have to wait until we get to heaven to live in God's power.

- The vision of a better future will help us pursue the change we need to make in our lives.

Discussion Questions

1. What are some ways your thinking has changed over the past few years?

2. Identify an undesirable behavior and consider what your life would be like without that behavior. What would be different if that behavior were under control?

3. Regarding the change you are pursuing in your life, write down the vision, intention, and means. If you lack any of these, consider talking through the issue with a close friend or family member.

4. How does God's kingdom power affect your approach to life?

5. What is your vision for a better future? Write it down and keep it posted in an area where you can see it regularly.

Chapter 19

DEVELOP
NEW HABITS

Once we have the vision to change and we understand the joy that's motivating us as followers of Christ, we should be the happiest, most joy-filled people on this planet. We should be happy and joy-filled because we know God has something better for us. A vision of the future, however, isn't enough. We need the intention to change. We need the intention that says, "I'm going to change. I'm deciding right now that I am changing."

Many of us fool ourselves by saying, "I'm going to change . . . I'm going to change . . . tomorrow. I'm going to change on Monday. I've got a vision, maybe a glimpse of it." Delayed obedience is disobedience. We can't just go through life acknowledging our need to change. Remember Josiah? He humbled himself, acted immediately, and had a responsive heart. Intention is part of acting now.

When we really have the intention to change, we say, "You know what? I have decided to make a difference. I am going to change." Now let me just say this for some of you who are a little worried right now. You might be thinking that this is sounding more and more like the self-help advice you'd hear on an afternoon television show. This isn't self-help. Self-help says, "I can do it on my own. There is no 'God-preferred' future out there." God-help says, "I can be renewed in my mind so that I can have life—life abundantly! I can do what God wants me to do." So, this is not just self-help here. This is a God-help strategy for us to apply in our lives.

We must ask God to give us the power and the grace to change. The beautiful thing is the Holy Spirit is working with us and in us and through us, helping us to achieve what Romans 12:1–2 tells us to do. We begin by letting God renew our minds. That causes us to think differently about everything. It's no longer about us; it's all about honoring God with our lives and doing what He has called us to do. When we live to please God, life just works. When we call ourselves believers and live in opposition to God, we've set ourselves up for a frustrating existence.

Philippians 2:13 says, "For it is God who works in you to will and to act according to His good purpose." So, He's helping you to work, He's helping you to change, He's helping you to get there. He's helping you say, "I'm going to do the right thing. I am going to change. I've got a vision of a better future. I've got a vision of where God wants me to be. I know where God wants me to go, and I want that! And, now, I have decided to change. I have the intention to change." But, how many of those words are followed with real change? Isn't it easy to make promises we never fulfill?

There's a saying that speaks to our intentions, "The road to hell is paved with good intentions." That's not in the Bible but it's a good saying! If you have the intention to change, you must decide to change and allow your actions to follow. Many people live with good intentions. They are going to change someday. They are going to do that someday. Tomorrow is the opportunity, but tomorrow never comes. Good intentions left undone are just random thoughts.

My wife does not like to be afraid. She especially does not like being scared at night. She used to watch shows like *CSI* when I was away. I'd come home and she would be afraid because of what she saw on television. She would say, "I'll save it until you're home and then we can watch it together." I asked, "Well, if you don't want to be afraid, why do you watch stuff like that?" Sometimes she would watch the show by peeking through her hands. I didn't understand, so I'd ask, "Well, why are you doing that?" She'd admit, "Well, I don't want to be afraid." I encouraged her to change, but she enjoyed parts of the show. It was a relentless battle between being entertained and being scared.

Self-help says, "I can do it on my own." God-help says, "I can do what God wants me to do."

Our decisions show if we're really serious. If we have the desire to change we need to say, "I've got the vision, I've got the intention, I'm going to change! I will change! This is going to be change for me! I'm doing it!" But even people who say that regularly find changing hard to do. You intend to do a lot of things. You intend to clean out the garage, go through your closet, have that physical you've put off for years. You intend to call a neighbor, go on a mission trip, give to your church. You have great intentions. But intentions alone aren't enough. You have to get to that moment that you know you're going to do it.

The best thing I can compare this to is when you are swimming and the water is cold. All of your friends are in the water, and they're asking you to jump in. You agree to jump in but in the process you chicken out, so they start teasing you. So you ask them to count to three and go to jump in, but you back off. Finally, you're serious this time, even though you've been faking it and backing out the other times. Something happens and you have the intention of jumping in this time, no kidding. Maybe your friends have given up on you but you haven't. This time you actually jump in. You have the vision and the intention to make it happen. It all helps you change before you have to. What else do you need?

You also need to have the means to change. The means to change is simply a way to accomplish what we say we want to do. It's the things we do, the decisions that lead to the actions, the things that we put in place in our life to change—the means. You can have intentions without means, but you'll never accomplish anything.

When God is alive in our lives and the change is according to His plan, we will have the means to change. God is working in us, but He doesn't work all by Himself in us. I don't know if you've ever prayed this prayer, but I've walked over to the piano and sat down and prayed, "God, I would just love to play the piano! That would be so cool if I could play the piano! And, if you could just give me that gift, I would love it!"

Afterward, when I tried to play the piano, the only sound I heard was *clank, clank, clank!* Apparently I didn't receive the gift. I have musical ability, but I don't know how to play the piano. Though God can change me and give me that ability, playing the piano is outside the scope of His plan for my life, and the only way I can learn to play it is by taking lessons and practicing!

Good intentions left undone are just random thoughts.

The change you are pursuing should be in line with God's best plan for you. He has wired you a specific way and equipped you with specific abilities. The better you know you, the better you can change so you can accomplish God's plans for your life.

Maybe you're saying, "God, I would love to lose forty pounds! I would love to lose forty pounds right now! And if you could just zap me, I'll hold my belt. Just go right ahead, just zap me! In Jesus name, amen! I have the faith of a mustard seed!" No you don't, you have the faith of a Big Mac! That's not how God works. He expects us to be participants in the change process. If He does it for us, we just keep asking for more and more. If we allow Him to work in us, to change us, our lives will reflect a spiritual vibrancy that is the by-product of God's presence and guidance in our lives.

Change isn't something God does to us; it's something God does through us. When you decide to change, you will need the vision, the intention, and the means to change. If you don't have those three elements, you will find yourself stuck in the place you are right now. That's the definition of insanity. You can't do what you're doing right now and become something you aren't.

If you keep doing what you're doing, you will be right where you are now next week, next month, and next year. Change isn't coming to find you. You must want it bad enough to do something about it. You have to make a choice.

Change before you have to.

CHAPTER 19 IN REVIEW

Key Ideas

◆ A vision of the future isn't enough. We need the intention to change.

◆ Self-help says, "I can do it on my own. There is no 'God-preferred' future out there." God-help says, "I can be renewed in my mind so that I can have life—life abundantly!"

◆ The Holy Spirit is working with us, in us, and through us, helping us to achieve what Romans 12:1–2 tells us to do.

◆ Our decisions show if we're really serious about changing.

◆ Change isn't something God does to us; it's something God does through us.

Discussion Questions

1. How would you rate your intention to change? Are there things you are more intentional about than you are about changing? Based on the intention you have, do you think change is possible?

2. Are you more dependent on self-help strategies or God-help strategies for change? What would your friends say about you in response to that question?

3. True believers depend on the Holy Spirit to accomplish change in their lives. What are three things you can do to become more dependent on the Holy Spirit?

4. Think back over the recent decisions you made regarding changes you want to experience. What do your decisions say about your intention to change?

5. We know that God changes us. What is your role in response to God's desire to change you?

Chapter 20

EXPECT GOD'S SPIRIT TO TRANSFORM YOU

God is working in you and through you, but He's also working with you! He's not leaving you on your own. He's working through you. He's doing this change through you, but you have to have the means to make the change. You have to start using His methods, His means, His practices. But, you also have to ask yourself, "What are the practices that I'm going to use to help bring about this change? God has given me the vision of a better future. I have the intention to do that—I have decided to do this. This time it's for real."

So, what are you going to do? What are the means by which you will achieve this change?

I believe there are some basic things all believers should do to prepare themselves for change. These things are the means to bring about the change. I always tell people to read the Bible, study the Bible, and allow God's Word to transform them into the people that He wants them to be. Are you going to start doing that? I encourage people to join a life group and start surrounding themselves with people who will support them and encourage them in their change.

Change is never easy, but it's almost impossible to change alone. We underestimate the importance of community, yet it was in community that the New Testament church was founded. In Acts 2:42–47, Luke tells us that the believers made being in community their number one priority. They ate together, studied Scripture together, shared possessions, and cared for one another. The Bible also tells us that, as a result of their commitment to each other, the church grew. People wanted to be a part of it. They saw the genuine community created by those believers, and they couldn't resist. It's too easy for people today to resist the church because the community in which it started has evaporated. Yet, community is important.

When you put yourself in the right situation, surrounded by people who are on your side, you'll discover that you can change. Researchers found that 77 percent of heart attack victims who joined a small group remained on track toward their life change because in a small group they had encouragement. This information comes from an article in *Fast Company*, "Change or Die," written by Alan Deutschman. It said that 77 percent of the people who had a positive view of the future, who had joy as their motivation, who joined a small group with other people sustained the change! Remember, this wasn't a Christian magazine. An article in a secular magazine reinforced what God's Word says! Here is how I advise people: "Read your Bible. Join a small group. Spend some time praying. Break free from the world's mindset! Get away from the bad thinking! Don't think like that anymore! Do the opposite of Hollywood! Go this way for God!" I implore them to do these things, not because I just want more people doing these things, but because these activities make the difference between thinking about change and actually changing! We tell people to take their thoughts captive. We tell people to memorize the Word of God. Some people will always push back, "Well, I can't do it." Yes you can! These are foundational things, these are not rocket science.

My workout regimen is not rocket science. If I would have just sat down and thought about it for just a few minutes, I could have done it. But I made excuses, "Oh, this is so complex." My trainer wouldn't hear it. He said, "No, this is basic. These are the things you need to do."

After he gave me the workout, my mind was changed. I remember saying, "Wow, that was so simple. Boy, am I ever dumb. Why didn't I think of the simple things?" When we look at God's Word, we see very clearly the simple things we're supposed to do to change. They're just so simple—there's no zapping going on right now. It's simple things that will bring about the change.

In the article "Change or Die" by *Fast Company*, the author stated that the people who just talked about change never changed. Heart attack victims who just said, "I've got a vision of a better future—I have *intention* to change" but never added the means, never really changed. You might be dabbling in change. Maybe you've been talking about it for a long time. You might have initiated some minor changes at some point, but you have never gotten really serious about changing. Heart attack victims who think this way will probably die before they engage in serious change.

The article talked about another group of heart attack victims who knew what they were supposed to do and made some changes. They said, "Oh, I can't eat this. And I've got to work out. And you know what, I need my sleep. And I've got to give up smoking. And I've got to . . ." They didn't just talk about change; they *did* what was necessary.

You see the difference, don't you? One group of people looked at all the things they needed to change and said, "I won't eat cheeseburgers. I'll eliminate cheeseburgers. Well, fries too. Cheeseburgers and fries and that dessert right there—I know that's my biggest problem. I won't eliminate these other things, I'm just going to eliminate cheeseburgers and fries and desserts sometimes."

They just dabbled with the idea of changing. The article said that these people were in the worst possible place. You know why? Because they hadn't accomplished enough change to really change their health, and they hadn't done enough change to really grab hold of the benefits of making good change. They continued living in the way they had always lived. They said, "I've changed and done enough, and I am okay." But they hadn't changed anything at all.

Now let me relate this to your spiritual life. God says, "I want you to

141

renew your mind. I want you to make these changes. I'll work with you! The Holy Spirit will work with you! I'll send a Comforter. He will lead you into all truth. He will be called alongside of you. He's going to help you! You've got him right beside you."

In response to God's offer, you might say, "All right, I've decided to follow Jesus." Then you look at the cost of following Jesus and something happens. You say, "Wow! Reading my Bible—all the time? Praying? Hmmm. And small group? Man, do I have to be part of the body of Christ? I need to be involved with other people and not be a lone ranger? What's this about tithing? I should obey God with my money and I should at least meet that Old Testament minimum standard?" Suddenly, the changes that accompany the decision are uncomfortable.

When we come face to face with God's expectations, we either yield to them or say, "Hmmm. I'll just attend church. Yeah, that's what I'll do. I'll attend church. The other stuff—that's optional. I'll just attend. As long as I attend, that's good. I won't serve, I won't do this whole list of things that will bring about change, I'm just going to do one thing."

You know what happens to people who try to do the minimum in their relationship with God? They're miserable! Miserable! That's right, they're miserable. You're wondering, "Why is my spiritual life dry? Why am I not having a breakthrough?" Because you're trying to meet the minimum standards.

You are guilty of saying something like, "I don't like *that* requirement, and I don't like *that* one, and especially not that one." You've picked only the things you like to do, those things that fit neatly into your previous lifestyle. You're fine with change just as long as you aren't the one needing to change.

Meanwhile, you're living in the same world as the guy who only got rid of the cheeseburger and fries. You think you've changed because you go to church and your friends don't go to church. You've fooled yourself into thinking, "That's all the change God wants me to do. That's all I need to do. I'm good." That's a lie. You won't feel good. You'll be miserable!

I'll just lay it out here: I think the Christian culture has convinced us that if we say the right things but don't do the right things, we're okay. As long as we've learned to speak Christianese, we're fine. "Pastor, bless God! Hallelujah! Repent! And be healed!" You've got it down, right? You know the phrases and the songs. You've got it! But, what happens when you return home?

Are you living with good intentions and good words but never applying any of God's truth to your life? You've never said, "I'm going to put in place the means to bring about a change of thinking because I know that my thinking is going to change, and I cannot be conformed to the world anymore!" And you've got to put those means in place! If you don't, you will be miserable!

I don't understand how you can call yourself a follower of Jesus Christ if you don't follow Jesus Christ! It has been long reported that Gandhi said something like, "The whole world would follow Jesus if Christians actually did what Jesus said!" But here's the problem: We've convinced ourselves that our intentions are good enough, our words are good enough, and we don't have to follow through with the means of doing it.

We've convinced ourselves that we're okay, but we're not. That is why the world looks at us and says, "Church? I don't need church! They're the same as me! They're not changing! There's no change in that life!"

People wake up to the reality of God when they see change in our lives. When you change, they say, "I knew you before. And you used to live like this. Look at you now. I don't even recognize you. Look at how different you are. What are you doing?" To which you can reply, "I'm changing! I'm being more like Jesus, that's what's happening. I'm really following Him. It's not just good intentions. I'm really doing this. I'm really changing. I'm really committed to what He wants me to do."

> I don't understand how you can call yourself a follower of Jesus Christ if you don't follow Jesus Christ!

I think there's a big challenge for all of us to get rid of our checklists and to embrace it all and to say, "I'm all in! God, I'm all in on the change you want in my life. I have a vision of what you want for me. I intend to do it. And I'll put the means in place right now to start renewing my mind and being the follower of Jesus Christ that I need to be."

The challenge is for all of us to stop picking and choosing what we like and saying we're all in. The people who are all in are the ones who have the joy of the Lord. They're the ones who are changing. You have the joy, you know it produces a life that is more abundant than anything you can imagine—a life full of abundance, passion, and satisfaction. That's what God wants for us!

So, we've got to change before we have to. We've got to change, but too many of us have snuck out without changing. Let me ask you something— Are you going to change before you have to? What tools are you going to put in place? What are you going to do differently now?

I pray that you'll just grab this—a vision for the future that God has for you. He has a better future for you. He does! He has a better future. His ways are higher than ours, they're significantly better. They may be tough, and many times they are. Tough, very tough—but always better. And you may say, "I'm happy now," but you have no idea of what you're missing out on. God wants you to be happy doing the obedient things, the tough things, and following His Word. Do that, have a vision for the future, the intention to change, and then put those means into place and you will change because the Holy Spirit is working with you to help you to renew your mind. You need to be transformed by the renewing of your mind. He's given us the tools to change, and it's up to us to change.

It all starts with following Jesus. Everything starts with following Jesus. You can't have a vision of a better future without Jesus. You may be a skinnier you. You may be a person who learns another language and that might make you feel good, but I'm telling you that the vision of the future God wants for you is for you to change and to say, "God, I accept You as my Lord and Savior, and I want to live for You. I want Your vision for my life."

As you read this today, perhaps you have come face to face with the reality that you've been living for yourself. The time is now for you to live for Jesus Christ. He is truth. He died on the cross for you. He rose again from the dead, and He is victorious! He is giving you the power to change, and He's asking you, "Will you change before you have to?"

The Bible says that "at the name of Jesus every knee should bow . . . and every tongue confess that Jesus Christ is Lord" (Phil. 2:10–11). And we get an opportunity to change before we have to. And there is going to be a day that you will be forced to admit that, and at that moment it will be too late. But here, right now, you can say, "I will change before I have to. I will take a knee." I will say, "Jesus, I confess my sins. I am sorry for my sins. I want to live for you for the rest of my life. And, God, Your plan will be my plan. I will be Your follower because You are true. You are Lord."

And I'm telling you—I want to change in every area of my life before I have to. Because there will be a day when all of us will have to admit that and say that and God wants us to change before we have to.

If you've never asked Jesus into your life, you can pray something like this:

"Dear Lord Jesus, I am sorry for my sins and everything I've done wrong. I ask for Your forgiveness and I thank You for Your forgiveness. You died on the cross and rose again, and I can have eternal life if I trust in You. I change now and become Your follower and will live for you for the rest of my life."

If you prayed that prayer, tell somebody you made the change. It's important that you do that. Call, text, or e-mail someone and say, "I had the intention. It wasn't just a good intention. I'm doing the means, and I'm telling someone about it now. I am going to put the means in place to make the change that I just did."

Change before you have to. Don't wait to change *because* you have to. The life you want—one of abundance, passion, and satisfaction—isn't out of reach if you'll decide to make the changes you've been on the fence about for too long. Stop stalling and start living with intention, purpose, and meaning. It will change your life—forever.

CHAPTER 20 IN REVIEW

Key Ideas

- God is working in you and through you, but He's also working with you!

- The best path to significant life change is to read the Bible, study the Bible, and allow God's Word to change you—to transform you—and to make you into the person that He wants you to be.

- People who decide to change but do nothing about it become miserable and frustrated with life.

- People wake up to the reality of God when they see change in our lives!

- The first change many people need to make is accepting Jesus as their personal Lord and Savior.

Discussion Questions

1. How is God working with you to navigate the change you need to make?

2. Are you reading and studying God's Word on your own? How is God transforming you through that process?

3. Describe a time when you decided to change but did nothing about it. How did you feel? What is different about this time?

4. What image of God is your life painting for others?

5. Briefly describe your salvation experience. How did you come to realize your need for a Savior? How has your life been changed since accepting Jesus Christ as your personal Lord and Savior?

CONCLUSION

Congratulations! You're reading this part of the book for one of two reasons: 1. You just finished reading through the book, or 2. you just flipped to the back to see if you could get a jump on the good stuff. (You're not the only one who likes to check out the end to see if the rest of the book is worth reading.)

I'm thrilled and delighted that you have picked up a copy of this book and invested the time and energy to read through it—or flip directly to the back. Wherever you are in life's journey, there are certainly things about your life that you'd like to change. You likely already know what those things are.

Once we decide to make the change and begin adjusting our lifestyles and choices to reflect our commitment to the change, the next most difficult step is to keep the change. You know what I'm talking about. You purchase the annual gym membership on December 15 and pay for an entire year to get the annual discount. You're completely convinced that you'll be able to make working out part of your normal routine. But March 1 rolls around and you realize you spent more days away from the gym than in the gym. You give up, and things go back to the way they were.

Don't you wish God included a button in the back of the Bible instead of the maps. Google has all the maps in the world. I want a button that I can press and ensure the changes I need to make happen—and stick. Unfortunately, that didn't happen.

Keeping the change is difficult—particularly if we aren't clear why we're doing it in the first place. But once we have a clear grasp on that, I think there are five things that will help you keep the change and avoid reverting back to old, destructive habits.

The first step is to be honest with yourself. The most difficult part about change is our refusal to accept that if we don't change, we could experience some very bad things. Our minds can confuse reality. It's easy for us to convince ourselves that things aren't as bad as some people make them out to be. If we aren't honest with ourselves, we'll never fully understand the need to change nor take personal ownership and responsibility to make the change.

The second step is to avoid the temptation to go halfway. Change is hard. We've discussed that throughout this book. It's the number one reason why so many give up and never fully make any changes to their lives. Once we decide to make the change, we can't go halfway. We must be all in. We must be committed to a better tomorrow. If we don't have a sense of what that "better tomorrow" is, then we won't have the strength to keep pushing forward when the difficult days come. And—yes—the difficult days will come.

The third step is to change for life, not for a season. Any living being is in the midst of constant change. We only stop changing when we die.

> The worst thing you could do is give up only a few days into implementing your change.

That means when we refuse to change, we deny who and how God created us as human beings. We should want to improve the conditions of our body—not just so we can look good on the beach but so that we will have the chance to hold our grandchildren in our arms. Even better, so we can see the fruit of our investment in others. Temporary change always leaves a bad taste in our mouths. I love it that my dad made changes in his life. Right before he died he told me, "I lived with no regrets." His changes were a huge investment in generations to follow.

The next step is to hold yourself accountable. This is a big one. A good management principle is, "What's measured gets managed." If no one is recording progress, then it's very easy to stop pushing and working to bring out the change that needs to take place. I would suggest that you share your thoughts, feelings, and decisions with your spouse, children, friends, and even your pastor. Find a few people who have earned the right to speak into your life and be honest with you. It will help you make the right decision in those hard moments.

The final step is to share your change with others. As part of holding yourself accountable, tell people around you—those outside your inner circle—about your decision. It will inspire them to think in similar ways about their lives, and it may give you the opportunity to share your change story. (Of course, I would love for you to share a copy of this book with them as well.) When we verbalize what's in our head, it becomes real. The change we make today is real, and we want to keep moving forward.

If you will incorporate these steps into your change process, you will have a much better chance of keeping the change you've committed to. The worst thing you could do is give up only a few days into implementing your change. I believe in you, and so does God. I know you have the power to change, and I want you to discover a life that is full of abundance, passion, and satisfaction.

The life you've always wanted isn't something for someone else. It can be yours. Stop listening to anyone who says it's impossible for you to successfully change. I'm a testimony to the contrary.

This is your opportunity to change. Don't let it go. Turn the page. Make your commitment real. Sign your name. And start change before you have to.

COMMIT TO KEEPING THE CHANGE

I want this book to represent a moment in your life when you started to live differently. I want you to write your initials next to the statements below as a sign of commitment and your first step in making the change before you have to. Then, I want you to take a few moments to record your first thoughts about personal change after having read this book. This is a great exercise to document your life choices and why you chose to change certain aspects of your life. Last, I want you to sign your name and date this page for future reference.

I will make the change before I have to because:

_____ I will be honest with myself

_____ I will not go halfway.

_____ I will change for life.

_____ I will hold myself accountable.

_____ I will share my change with others.

I commit to this change:

I am making this commitment because:

I will do these things to ensure I keep the change:

My signature below represents my personal commitment to make the change before I have to. As often as I reflect on this day and the circumstances surrounding my decision to change, I will remember the commitment I made with myself, those whom I love, those who love me, and especially with God who will give me the strength to endure until the change is complete.

_____ (Signature)

_____ (Date)

FURTHER READING

10 Faith-Based Books

1. *The Purpose-Driven Life* by Rick Warren
2. *Let God Change Your Life: How to Know and Follow Jesus* by Greg Laurie
3. *The Me I Want to Be* by John Ortberg
4. *Unstuck: Your Life. God's Design. Real Change.* by Michael Ross and Arnie Cole
5. *The Miracle of Life Change: How God Transforms His Children* by Chip Ingram
6. *Boundaries: When to Say YES, When to Say NO, To Take Control of Your Life* by Henry Cloud and John Townsend
7. *The 24-Hour Turn-Around: Change Your Life One Hour at a Time* by Neil Eskelin and Jim Hartness
8. *A Life-Changing Encounter with God's Word from the Book of Proverbs* by The Navigators
9. *The God I Never Knew: How Real Friendship with the Holy Spirit Can Change Your Life* by Robert Morris
10. *You Can Change: God's Transforming Power for Our Sinful Behavior and Negative Emotions* by Tim Cheste

10 Non Faith-Based Books

1. *Change Anything* by Kerry Patterson, Joseph Grenny, David Maxfield, Ron McMillan, Al Switzler
2. *Becoming a Life Change Artist: 7 Creative Skills to Reinvent Yourself at Any Stage of Life* by Fred Mandell and Kathleen Jordan
3. *Saying Yes to Change: 10 Timeless Life Lessons for Creating Positive Change* by Alex Blackwell

4. *The Power of Habit: Why We Do What We Do in Life and Business* by Charles Duhigg
5. *Be Fearless: Change Your Life in 28 Days* by Jonathan Alpert and Alisa Bowman
6. *Across That Bridge* by John Lewis
7. *Change Your Life in 30 Days: A Journey to Finding Your True Self* by Rhonda Britten
8. *Coach Wooden: The 7 Principles that Shaped His Life and Will Change Yours* by Pat Williams and James Denney
9. *Do One Thing Different: Ten Simple Ways to Change Your Life* by William Hudson O'Hanlon
10. *Rewire Your Brain: Think Your Way to a Better Life* by John B. Arden

SCRIPTURE GUIDE FOR PERSONAL DEVOTION

REFERENCE	VERSE
Psalm 25:8–10	Good and upright is the LORD; therefore he instructs sinners in his ways. He guides the humble in what is right and teaches them his way. All the ways of the LORD are loving and faithful toward those who keep the demands of his covenant.
John 15:5–8	I am the vine; you are the branches. If you remain in me and I in you, you will bear much fruit; apart from me you can do nothing. If you do not remain in me, you are like a branch that is thrown away and withers; such branches are picked up, thrown into the fire and burned. If you remain in me and my words remain in you, ask whatever you wish, and it will be done for you. This is to my Father's glory, that you bear much fruit, showing yourselves to be my disciples.
Rom. 6:12–14	Therefore do not let sin reign in your mortal body so that you obey its evil desires. Do not offer any part of yourself to sin as an instrument of wickedness, but rather offer yourselves to God as those who have been brought from death to life; and offer every part of yourself to him as an instrument of righteousness. For sin shall no longer be your master, because you are not under the law, but under grace.

REFERENCE	VERSE
Rom. 8:5–11	Those who live according to the flesh have their minds set on what the flesh desires; but those who live in accordance with the Spirit have their minds set on what the Spirit desires. The mind governed by the flesh is death, but the mind governed by the Spirit is life and peace. The mind governed by the flesh is hostile to God; it does not submit to God's law, nor can it do so. Those who are in the realm of the flesh cannot please God. You, however, are not in the realm of the flesh but are in the realm of the Spirit, if indeed the Spirit of God lives in you. And if anyone does not have the Spirit of Christ, they do not belong to Christ. But if Christ is in you, then even though your body is subject to death because of sin, the Spirit gives life because of righteousness. And if the Spirit of him who raised Jesus from the dead is living in you, he who raised Christ from the dead will also give life to your mortal bodies because of his Spirit who lives in you.
Rom. 8:28	And we know that in all things God works for the good of those who love him, who have been called according to his purpose.
Rom. 12:1–2	Therefore, I urge you, brothers and sisters, in view of God's mercy, to offer your bodies as a living sacrifice, holy and pleasing to God—this is your true and proper worship. Do not conform to the pattern of this world, but be transformed by the renewing of your mind. Then you will be able to test and approve what God's will is —his good, pleasing and perfect will.

REFERENCE	VERSE
Rom. 12:17–21	Do not repay anyone evil for evil. Be careful to do what is right in the eyes of everyone. If it is possible, as far as it depends on you, live at peace with everyone. Do not take revenge, my dear friends, but leave room for God's wrath, for it is written: "It is mine to avenge; I will repay," says the Lord. On the contrary: "If your enemy is hungry, feed him; if he is thirsty, give him something to drink. In doing this, you will heap burning coals on his head." Do not be overcome by evil, but overcome evil with good.
Rom. 13:8–10	Let no debt remain outstanding, except the continuing debt to love one another, for whoever loves others has fulfilled the law. The commandments, "You shall not commit adultery," "You shall not murder," "You shall not steal," "You shall not covet," and whatever other command there may be, are summed up in this one command: "Love your neighbor as yourself." Love does no harm to a neighbor. Therefore love is the fulfillment of the law.
Rom. 13:13–14	Let us behave decently, as in the daytime, not in carousing and drunkenness, not in sexual immorality and debauchery, not in dissension and jealousy. Rather, clothe yourselves with the Lord Jesus Christ, and do not think about how to gratify the desires of the flesh.
Gal. 5:13–15	You, my brothers and sisters, were called to be free. But do not use your freedom to indulge the flesh; rather, serve one another humbly in love. For the entire law is fulfilled in keeping this one command: "Love your neighbor as yourself." If you bite and devour each other, watch out or you will be destroyed by each other.

REFERENCE	VERSE
Gal. 5:22–25	But the fruit of the Spirit is love, joy, peace, forbearance, kindness, goodness, faithfulness, gentleness and self-control. Against such things there is no law. Those who belong to Christ Jesus have crucified the flesh with its passions and desires. Since we live by the Spirit, let us keep in step with the Spirit.
Eph. 4:1–3	As a prisoner for the Lord, then, I urge you to live a life worthy of the calling you have received. Be completely humble and gentle; be patient, bearing with one another in love. Make every effort to keep the unity of the Spirit through the bond of peace.
Eph. 5:1–5	Follow God's example, therefore, as dearly loved children and walk in the way of love, just as Christ loved us and gave himself up for us as a fragrant offering and sacrifice to God. But among you there must not be even a hint of sexual immorality, or of any kind of impurity, or of greed, because these are improper for God's holy people. Nor should there be obscenity, foolish talk or coarse joking, which are out of place, but rather thanksgiving. For of this you can be sure: No immoral, impure or greedy person—such a person is an idolater —has any inheritance in the kingdom of Christ and of God.
Eph. 5:15–17	Be very careful, then, how you live —not as unwise but as wise, making the most of every opportunity, because the days are evil. Therefore do not be foolish, but understand what the Lord's will is.

REFERENCE	VERSE
Eph. 6:10–17	Finally, be strong in the Lord and in his mighty power. Put on the full armor of God, so that you can take your stand against the devil's schemes. For our struggle is not against flesh and blood, but against the rulers, against the authorities, against the powers of this dark world and against the spiritual forces of evil in the heavenly realms. Therefore put on the full armor of God, so that when the day of evil comes, you may be able to stand your ground, and after you have done everything, to stand. Stand firm then, with the belt of truth buckled around your waist, with the breastplate of righteousness in place, and with your feet fitted with the readiness that comes from the gospel of peace. In addition to all this, take up the shield of faith, with which you can extinguish all the flaming arrows of the evil one. Take the helmet of salvation and the sword of the Spirit, which is the word of God.
Phil. 1:21	For to me, to live is Christ and to die is gain.
Phil. 1:27–30	Whatever happens, conduct yourselves in a manner worthy of the gospel of Christ. Then, whether I come and see you or only hear about you in my absence, I will know that you stand firm in the one Spirit, striving together as one for the faith of the gospel without being frightened in any way by those who oppose you. This is a sign to them that they will be destroyed, but that you will be saved— and that by God. For it has been granted to you on behalf of Christ not only to believe in him, but also to suffer for him, since you are going through the same struggle you saw I had, and now hear that I still have.
Phil. 2:3–4	Do nothing out of selfish ambition or vain conceit. Rather, in humility value others above yourselves, not looking to your own interests but each of you to the interests of the others.

REFERENCE	VERSE
Phil. 2:14–16	Do everything without grumbling or arguing, so that you may become blameless and pure, "children of God without fault in a warped and crooked generation." Then you will shine among them like stars in the sky as you hold firmly to the word of life. And then I will be able to boast on the day of Christ that I did not run or labor in vain.
Phil. 4:6–7	Do not be anxious about anything, but in every situation, by prayer and petition, with thanksgiving, present your requests to God. And the peace of God, which transcends all understanding, will guard your hearts and your minds in Christ Jesus.
Phil. 4:13	I can do all this through him who gives me strength.
Col. 2:6–7	So then, just as you received Christ Jesus as Lord, continue to live your lives in him, rooted and built up in him, strengthened in the faith as you were taught, and overflowing with thankfulness.
Col. 2:8–11	See to it that no one takes you captive through hollow and deceptive philosophy, which depends on human tradition and the elemental spiritual forces of this world rather than on Christ. For in Christ all the fullness of the Deity lives in bodily form, and in Christ you have been brought to fullness. He is the head over every power and authority. In him you were also circumcised with a circumcision not performed by human hands. Your whole self ruled by the flesh was put off when you were circumcised by Christ,

REFERENCE	VERSE
Col. 3:1–4	Since, then, you have been raised with Christ, set your hearts on things above, where Christ is, seated at the right hand of God. Set your minds on things above, not on earthly things. For you died, and your life is now hidden with Christ in God. When Christ, who is your life, appears, then you also will appear with him in glory.
Col. 3:5–11	Put to death, therefore, whatever belongs to your earthly nature: sexual immorality, impurity, lust, evil desires and greed, which is idolatry. Because of these, the wrath of God is coming. You used to walk in these ways, in the life you once lived. But now you must also rid yourselves of all such things as these: anger, rage, malice, slander, and filthy language from your lips. Do not lie to each other, since you have taken off your old self with its practices and have put on the new self, which is being renewed in knowledge in the image of its Creator. Here there is no Gentile or Jew, circumcised or uncircumcised, barbarian, Scythian, slave or free, but Christ is all, and is in all.
James 1:5	If any of you lacks wisdom, you should ask God, who gives generously to all without finding fault, and it will be given to you.
James 1:12	Blessed is the one who perseveres under trial because, having stood the test, that person will receive the crown of life that the Lord has promised to those who love him.
James 1:19–21	My dear brothers and sisters, take note of this: Everyone should be quick to listen, slow to speak and slow to become angry, because human anger does not produce the righteousness that God desires. Therefore, get rid of all moral filth and the evil that is so prevalent and humbly accept the word planted in you, which can save you.

REFERENCE	VERSE
James 1:22–25	Do not merely listen to the word, and so deceive yourselves. Do what it says. Anyone who listens to the word but does not do what it says is like someone who looks at his face in a mirror and, after looking at himself, goes away and immediately forgets what he looks like. But whoever looks intently into the perfect law that gives freedom, and continues in it—not forgetting what they have heard, but doing it—they will be blessed in what they do.
James 5:7–8	Be patient, then, brothers and sisters, until the Lord's coming. See how the farmer waits for the land to yield its valuable crop, patiently waiting for the autumn and spring rains. You too, be patient and stand firm, because the Lord's coming is near.
James 5:17–18	Elijah was a human being, even as we are. He prayed earnestly that it would not rain, and it did not rain on the land for three and a half years. Again he prayed, and the heavens gave rain, and the earth produced its crops.
1 Pet. 1:13–16	Therefore, with minds that are alert and fully sober, set your hope on the grace to be brought to you when Jesus Christ is revealed at his coming. As obedient children, do not conform to the evil desires you had when you lived in ignorance. But just as he who called you is holy, so be holy in all you do; for it is written: "Be holy, because I am holy."
1 Pet. 4:7–8	The end of all things is near. Therefore be alert and of sober mind so that you may pray. Above all, love each other deeply, because love covers over a multitude of sins.

REFERENCE	VERSE
1 Pet. 4:10	Each of you should use whatever gift you have received to serve others, as faithful stewards of God's grace in its various forms.
1 Pet. 4:12–14	Dear friends, do not be surprised at the fiery ordeal that has come on you to test you, as though something strange were happening to you. But rejoice inasmuch as you participate in the sufferings of Christ, so that you may be overjoyed when his glory is revealed. If you are insulted because of the name of Christ, you are blessed, for the Spirit of glory and of God rests on you.
1 Pet. 5:6–7	Humble yourselves, therefore, under God's mighty hand, that he may lift you up in due time. Cast all your anxiety on him because he cares for you.
1 Pet. 5:8–9	Be alert and of sober mind. Your enemy the devil prowls around like a roaring lion looking for someone to devour. Resist him, standing firm in the faith, because you know that the family of believers throughout the world is undergoing the same kind of sufferings.
2 Pet. 1:3–4	His divine power has given us everything we need for a godly life through our knowledge of him who called us by his own glory and goodness. Through these he has given us his very great and precious promises, so that through them you may participate in the divine nature, having escaped the corruption in the world caused by evil desires.

WHERE TO GO FOR HELP

Note: Please know this list is not exhaustive. It is meant to be a place to start.

ALCOHOLISM

Name: Alcoholics Anonymous
Website: http://www.aa.org/
Description: Alcoholics Anonymous is an international fellowship of men and women who share their experience, strength, and hope with each other in order to solve their common problem and help others to recover from alcoholism.

Name: Sober.com
Website: http://www.sober.com/
Description: Sober.com is an online resource dedicated to fighting the stigma and the disease of alcoholism by providing education, information, help, and hope. They provide information for treatment centers, halfway houses, and other community resources for alcoholics.

PORNOGRAPHY

Name: XXX Church and X3 Watch
Website: http://xxxchurch.com/
Description: X3 Watch is a free accountability software program offered by XXXchurch.com. Whenever you visit a questionable site, X3 Watch saves the site name on the computer and sends a report to your selected accountability partners.

Name: Pure Intimacy

Website: www.pureintimacy.org

Description: A website for those struggling to overcome online pornography, as well as spouses of those struggling, sponsored by Focus on the Family.

Name: The Helpline for Pornography Addiction

Number: 1-800-583-2964

Description: Sponsored by the National Coalition for the Protection of Children and Families, the helpline provides trained counselors available during business hours to help individuals addicted to pornography as well as the spouses of those addicted.

DEPRESSION

Name: Mental Health America

Website: www.nmha.org

Description: Mental Health America is a leading nonprofit group that supports good mental health for all people. On the web site, you can access information on mental health topics, depending on ethnic group, career or military, and age group.

DRUG ABUSE

Name: Addiction Treatment Forum

Website: http://www.atforum.com/

Description: The Addiction Treatment Forum is an educational site focusing on addiction issues, especially opiate addiction and treatment. The site provides books, a clinic locator, and an open forum for those dealing with drug abuse.

CAREER

Name: National Career Development Association
Website: http://associationdatabase.com
Description: NCDA provides programs and services for career development professionals and for the public involved with or interested in career development, including, but not limited to, professional development activities, publications, research, general information, professional standards, advocacy, and recognition for achievement and service.

Name: What Color Is Your Parachute?
Website: http://www.jobhuntersbible.com/
Description: *What Color Is Your Parachute?* is a personal career workbook that will help you identify the best career for your personality and gifts. The site also provides a plethora of information on different career choices as well as insights on getting into your preferred career field.

FAMILY

Name: Focus on the Family
Website: http://www.focusonthefamily.com/
Description: Focus on the Family is a global Christian ministry dedicated to helping families thrive. The organization provides help and resources for couples to build healthy marriages, and for parents to raise their children according to morals and values grounded in biblical principles. Their website provides thousands of resources and articles to help you improve the life and well-being of your family.

Name: Smalley Center
Website: http://smalley.cc/
Description: The Smalley Center is a Christian marriage ministry proven to help couples in difficult situations. The organization has developed an intensive program to help couples recover their marriage. The

Smalley Center provides the best, licensed Christian marriage counselors and psychologists who are passionate about doing intensive counseling and who are willing to partner with individuals to reach hurting couples. They currently have locations in Houston, Dallas, Shreveport, Nashville, and Branson.

Name: Cross Walk
Website: http://www.crosswalk.com
Description: Cross Walk is a for-profit organization that helps parents and families improve their relationships. The resource provides devotionals, resources, videos, and podcasts in an effort to help parents lead their families the best way possible.

EATING DISORDERS

Name: Academy for Eating Disorders
Website: http://www.aedweb.org
Description: The Academy for Eating Disorders is a multidisciplinary association of academic and clinical professionals with demonstrated interest and expertise in the field of eating disorders.

Name: Something Fishy
Website: http://www.something-fishy.org/
Description: Something Fishy is a website for those struggling with eating disorders. The site provides a great deal of information on the various eating disorders, a quiz to help you determine if you struggle with an eating disorder, as well as numerous information on organizations to contact for those struggling with the disease.

MONEY

Name: Financial Peace University
Website: http://www.daveramsey.com/fpu

Description: Financial Peace University is a money and debt management training course provided by Dave Ramsey. Financial Peace University resources are often provided through local churches, banks, correction facilities, and nonprofits.

Name: My Money Management
Website: http://www.mymoneymanagement.net/
Description: My Money Management provides some of the best information, tools, and resources to tackle challenges like managing debt. The organization also provides resources on financial counseling, insights on making money decisions and meeting your goals, and financial education worksheets.

MISCELLANEOUS

Name: I Am Second
Website: http://www.iamsecond.com
Description: I Am Second is a movement meant to inspire people of all kinds to live for God and for others. The authentic stories on iamsecond.com provide insight into dealing with typical struggles of everyday living. These are stories that give hope to the lonely and the hurting, help from destructive lifestyles, and inspiration to the unfulfilled.

Name: You're On! App
Website: https://www.changeanything.com/
Description: In conjunction with the book *Change Anything*, the You're On! App helps users escape the false notion that willpower alone is required to make change stick and helps them become both the subject and scientist of the dynamics of their own behavior. Users compete with friends to see who can complete the most challenges, but ultimately all this fun is designed to keep people motivated to reach their life-change goals.

Name: Celebrate Recovery

Website: www.celebraterecovery.com

Description: Celebrate Recovery is a program designed to help those struggling with hurts, hang-ups, and habits by showing them the loving power of Jesus Christ through the recovery process.

Name: Teen Challenge

Website: www.teenchallengeusa.com

Description: Teen Challenge provides youth adults and families with an effective and comprehensive Christian faith-based solution to life-controlling drug and alcohol problems in order to become productive members of society. By applying biblical principles, Teen Challenge endeavors to help people become mentally-sound, emotionally-balanced, socially-adjusted, physically-well, and spiritually-alive.

ABOUT THE AUTHOR

Rob Ketterling is the founder and Lead Pastor of River Valley Church (rivervalleychurch.org), a multisite church started in Minnesota in 1995. It has since grown into a thriving church with over 5,000 in attendance across five U.S. campuses and one international campus in Valencia, Spain, with further expansion plans in its future. Through his unique, practical preaching style, vision casting and gifts of leadership, Rob encourages people to live out River Valley's mission of cultivating an authentic, life-changing relationship with Jesus Christ. Rob serves on several church and parachurch boards and the Board of Regents at North Central University and is on the Lead Team of the Association of Related Churches (ARC). Rob and his wife, Becca, live in Minnesota with their two boys Connor and Logan. You can follow Rob on Twitter (@robketterling), Facebook (robketterling), and through his blog (robketterling.com).

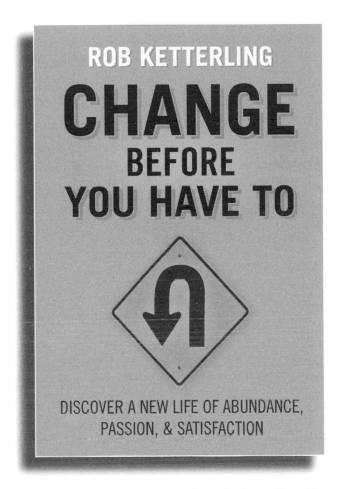

To order more copies of this book please visit
www.influenceresources.com